Running
&
Breathing

Running
&
Breathing

Justin O'Brien, Ph.D.

Yes International Publishers
Saint Paul, Minnesota 55105

Yes International Publishers
1317 Summit Avenue
Saint Paul, MN 55105-2602
651-645-6808
www.yespublishers.com

Library of Congress Control Number: 20021067729
ISBN: 0-936663-29-4

Printed in the United States of America

To Devi
whose spirit runs to the stars!

In Appreciation

Without the unselfish efforts of many people, this book would not have been completed. I would especially like to thank my friends, Wally Bernstein, M.D. and David Coulter, Ph.D. for their technical assistance in biology. I am grateful to Lorraine Wells for her fine, creative drawings of yoga postures and human anatomy, to Nancy Avery for the clear graph designs, and to Anton Crane for the splendid cover.

Table of Contents

Introduction

Christmas week was quiet and not very cold. Hardly any snow had fallen this December. Looking out my office window, my thoughts went back to the summer months, when just about everyone was jogging. I remembered how on a few occasions the urge to join them surfaced, but the feeling soon lost its urgency once I remembered the sore legs, the burning lungs, and the other discomforts associated with the training programs of my school days.

I had always enjoyed running throughout most of my life. Until the present sedentary years, I experimented with many approaches to training. Although I could feel the healthful benefits of improved fitness, the harsh demands upon my body soon eclipsed the enjoyment of running itself and my interest faded. I knew that something was missing from these standard approaches, but I could not put my finger on it.

So, looking out upon the leafless trees, I put the thought of running from my mind. The wind died down and a light snow began to fall softly. Unable to resist the atmosphere, I bundled up for a walk. It was one of those rare evenings when the combination of the coolness and calmness allowed one to listen to the snow's alighting. I wanted to stay out and walk for hours. Before long my thoughts returned again to running. Only this time my mind began to make associations that surprised me. I started to conceive a plan.

Could it be possible that a new ground in running be explored? I thought of all the benefits of my yoga practices, and realized that the practice of controlled breathing and meditation had had the most benefit on my life in terms of health and growth. Why not experiment with an approach to running built around the breath? Could one run and train by using these methods? The approach, as far as I knew, was untried. Who could say whether it was feasible or even possible?

Walking along in the dark night air the ideas kept surfacing. Why not bring in a holistic approach to the plan, along with specific breathing methods? Why not experiment and see if the application can be broadened and become the basis for running for a lifetime? Are there universal factors in running regardless of age or condition? Are these same factors flexible enough for people to compose their own running program or workouts to suit their needs and abilities? What I wanted to explore with myself was a method of running that could be enjoyable and useful at any age.

I began to experiment. The experiment succeeded with each passing month. I found that I could run with increasing fitness without straining the muscles or even getting out of breath. Speed came as endurance grew. By the end of the year, running for one hour was common. The body never was taxed to fatigue. The rhythmic breathing sustained the pace but never left me breathless.

As a professional lecturer, I have traveled to many cities over the years. These opportunities have enabled me to teach this program to many. It was divided into topics that have a direct bearing upon the method; diet, stretching, the functioning of the heart and lungs, the healing and prevention of injuries – all these aspects are treated from the perspective of building a lifelong program of enjoyable running. The principles found in the text apply equally whether one jogs at a pace of fifteen minutes per mile or is attempting to reach a racing level. Age is no barrier. It is my hope that this book will help you to recover your natural state of fitness through running while enjoying the recovery.   JOB

1
Why Run?

C onsider a common crisis situation in the Western world today: an individual over thirty is overweight and short of breath. Add the following statistics: his cholesterol count is consistently over 300, triglycerides 400, blood pressure 150, and resting pulse 85 beats per minute. This description resembles the average middle-aged man in America. He can barely run a short distance without feeling tremendous fatigue. Unknown to him, that same short distance measures how far he is from a serious heart attack.

Here is the same person six months later: weight is now 25 pounds less, blood pressure is 125/80, resting pulse is 68 and cholesterol and triglycerides are both under 200. No drugs produced these changes, no special therapy, no radical changes in diet. These astonishing improvements in the vital signs of life came about because this person wanted them. He became a runner.

In our ambition to succeed at our life work, we often slack off in caring for our health. The recipient of this neglect is our body. The body is very forgiving—it compensates for our neglect again and again. If the neglect is constant, however, the body soon reminds us of the high price we have paid. We become ill. We just don't fall out of good condition; we have to decide to do so. We must continually renew our decision to remain out of condition. We constantly refuse to allow a sustainable program of intelligent exercise to become a part of our lifestyle. If we are convinced that exercise does not matter, then the consequences of our conviction are included in the goal of our life.

We cannot escape our decisions. The attitude of indifference is also a decision, complete with its own consequences. To stay on the sidelines regarding the argument about exercise benefits being worth the trouble or not does not let us off the hook. Our daily living is a constant renewal of the decision to live in a certain way. Like it or not, a long as we are alive, each day demands a re-creation of the kind of bodily lifestyle that we have chosen for ourselves.

One's lifestyle implies either the promotion or undermining of health and well-being. To some extent, these two items are an endowment. As I get older, their continued presence becomes riskier. I forget that the arrival of bad health in middle or late years is not a sudden, automatic appearance; it is something that has been forged daily over many years. Hundreds upon hundreds of choices have resulted in the state of my health. I have not evolved to my current level of fitness in some mysterious, impersonal way. What I have done with my endowment is strictly my personal responsibility. For the most part, I have no one to praise or blame but myself.

Primitive animal life in the woods or jungle is basically instinctual. Choice is not a factor for survival. Under those circumstances, the level of health can be laid more directly at nature's feet. Unlike most of nature's creatures, however, the human is an exception. Together with instinct and obedience to the laws of nature, humans also have rational choice. That is why a human can outrun animals, not in swiftness but endurance. These two factors, instinct and decision, comprise our endowment for well or ill living. How we use the body determines what the body becomes for our future.

It may seem strange to look upon health primarily as a decision. Just as we choose the type and amount of diet, so we choose whether or not to exercise and how much to do so. No doubt health is a complex of many factors, including diet, reaction, attitude, geography, and cultural conditions. But the ability to choose gives man the edge in nature's kingdom. Other animals have to put up with their physical endowment alone. We human beings have the option to make a difference with our endowment. We can improve it.

When we exercise a choice, however insignificant, we are acting humanly. When we choose to exercise by running, we are creating those conditions which can improve the quality of our life.

Running can stimulate the entire endowment of life both directly and indirectly. Through running we are better prepared to face life's challenges physically, mentally, and emotionally. Our vitality is enriched and strengthened.

Running does not have to be a harsh experience of sore muscles and breathless feelings. Approached with patience and imagination, running can instead generate a new state of well-being.

Exercising the body properly, feeling the increased sense of satisfaction has rewards that contribute to all areas of life. Talk to runners who enjoy running for its own sake and they will tell you that its benefits enhance the normal duties of life.

For some, getting through their daily running has given them a lift in self-confidence which affects other areas of personal and career involvement. The practical test of your workout is simply to note how you feel when it is over.

The human organism is so uniquely integrated that when an activity improves some aspects of it, the other parts or dimensions share in the achievement.

When someone learns how to run well, it benefits the entire health of the person beyond the ambit of running.

Running Develops Confidence

Running produces an experience that brings about a greater sense of self-confidence. Many goals in life are beyond our exclusive control; many demand external accessories for their completion. Running is not one of them. Running, like walking, is available to anyone, to both genders and at just about any age or time of the year. The runner is self-determined. The consequences of one's workout are the products of one's own choice. The runner is a self-made artist, a creator of conditions in which body and mind are the active recipients of inspiration and labor. S/he defies the laws of inertia and uses energy to enlarge the capacity for life. The runner expands the creation of the endowment, forcing time to become an ally.

All of these discoveries inspire the runner to a new sense of confidence; condition and confidence go together. The human organism is so generous that it has healthful potentials most people rarely reach. Over a period of weeks the stimulation of running awakens these healthful reserves. The runner actually incorporates these reserves into the overall makeup of his well-being. The sense of achievement which results becomes the basis for self-confidence. In this way, the better the conditioning the stronger the confidence.

One runner interviewed in *Woman Runner* says,

> Running has given me a purpose, a sense of self. It has opened numerous doors of learning about diet, anatomy, and psychology. Running has helped me to like people again through learning to like myself. It has given me a pride in self...I had forgotten I possessed.

Running Develops Endurance

Life's tasks are so much easier when one can take its challenges in stride. It is difficult to accept new challenges, however, when one's fatigue threshold is reached early in the game. Becoming easily tired is discouraging.

This running program promotes health from the perspective of developing endurance. Since it is a load-bearing exercise, running calls certain major parts of the body and extremities repeatedly into play. It is this sustained repetition over a period of time that forges the development of endurance. Dr. Ernest von Aaken, who has coached world record holders, points out that, "Endurance is acquired mainly by prolonged exercise done at a moderate tempo." It is amazing when one considers this simple formula: steady, repetitious running builds healthful endurance. Intelligent use of energy begets more energy.

In contrast, our everyday use of the world of metals, glass, and plastics leads to their breakdown. Driving your car wears it out. No matter how careful you are about material things, using them does not expand their reserves nor strengthen their performance. But when it comes to running, the human body decidedly improves itself with use. Steady, repetitious running increases health. It reduces fatigue and allows the body to build up its recuperative powers. While building a base of endurance, a runner surpasses his former physical boundaries. The body's endurance grows even if you don't believe in the possibility. Your heart rate, your metabolism, your oxygen utilization, all improve their capacity with easy running. Do you get tired as quickly now as you did in the first few days? You will have to say "no". You are now on the way to building endurance.

Running Relieves Depression

Sometimes we find an event in life that saddens and depresses us. We can't help brooding over it, often for long periods. This sadness saps our energy and leaves us unsure of how to help oneself out of the depression. Depression is an internal condition; thus, the dynamics for relieving this state of affairs can start with an activity that is inherently designed to improve health.

Just as the mind influences the body, so the body's condition influences the mind; there is a reciprocal relationship easily verified

in everyday life. If a sad thought lingers in your mind, it has a debilitating effect upon your body. Your countenance, your posture, your
appetite for food or recreation, even your speech, reveal the physical
counterpart of the sadness. Certain chemical and electromagnetic
changes occur since the body wants to follow the lead of the depressed
mind. We never say, "My body is cheerful, but my mind is sad."

While many therapies attempt to resolve the problem of depression through a mental approach, they will not be fully successful if
they ignore the body. While negative thoughts can disturb the body's
healthful operation, often leading to serious illness, the opposite is
equally true.

When embarking on improving the body's fitness, if one can moderate negative feelings, depression will often dissolve. As the body
becomes healthier the mind is disposed toward more positive
thoughts. It is not surprising, then, to find that running has something to contribute to the problem of relieving depression. Through
the years, runners have discovered that their minor anxieties, which
drain so much of their energy, seem to melt away during their workouts. Anger and sadness can be effectively lessened through the rhythmic activity of running. The sense of accomplishment, the physical
pleasure, the alteration of the energy into a balanced mood produced
by running, "picks up" the person and makes him/her feel better.

Dr. John Griest and his colleagues at the University of Wisconsin
have been experimenting with running in conjunction with psy-
chotherapy as a primary treatment for clinical depression. An article
in *Behavioral Medicine,* by Dr. Griest reports on their work in this
field. "The goal of the running therapy was not to cover a particular
distance at a set pace. We felt that impressive personal performances
and improved mood would follow naturally along if patients became
regular runners." In the summary of a ten-week therapy session, with
eight patients being treated for moderate depression, they report that
six of the eight patients had recovered from their depression after a

program of running. Dr. Griest also mentions a study he conducted of 167 college students diagnostically tested for depression levels. The students were asked to exercise three times a week for eight weeks, choosing either wrestling, tennis, varied exercises, jogging, or softball. After the eight-week interval, the joggers showed the greatest reduction in depression scores.

Among other improvements, these runners were beginning to increase their endurance. When an organism increases its endurance, it improves its ability to function optimally under pressure. When one feels better, one works better, and life is fresher and less fatiguing. All the systems of the body get toned up. One feels a surge of vitality. Feeling better, one can't help but look at life's future a little more optimistically. Feeling consistently well is an endowment that we often abuse. Running is an opportunity to recover the way we should feel in facing life.

Running Reduces Stress

Stress has many faces. Hypertension, melancholy, headache, a general feeling of sadness or anxiety are some of the more familiar signs by which we recognize this condition. Stress is not respectful of social or educational advantages in society; it affects everyone. But these afflictions are not invading the person ab extra, from external sources. Someone undergoing the stress of worry, for example, generates the condition for himself, ab intra.

Dr. Phil Nuernberger, in his excellent book, *Freedom from Stress,* points out:

> Stress is more than being "up tight" occasionally or having a bad day. It is a recurring imbalance resulting in the daily wear and tear on the body that leads to dysfunction and debilitation. It comes in different guises. Emotional stress (or mental stress) is the stress generated by our personality as we interact with our environment on a day-to-day basis

(this sometimes referred to as social stress). Digestive stress is the stress that we get from poor eating habits. Environmental stress is created by such factors as smog, noise and air pollution. The reason stress is harmful is because we are unconsciously creating it and we become accustomed to sustaining it. Consequently we come to accept stress as a "normal" part of everyday life.

Granted a certain foundational wellness within the person, the exact causes of stressful feelings may not be obvious to the sufferer. If one is frequently finding himself in a less than optimal mood of calm energy to perform the normal tasks of career and daily living, there may yet be a comfortable way to lessen the occurrence. Take up running. Drs. P. Insel and W. Roth of Stanford University agree that, "The most profound muscular and mental relaxation cannot be achieved by just trying to relax. The deepest relaxation, as measured by electrodes inserted in the muscles, follows a period of voluntary increased muscle tension."

Many runners testify that something positive, a feeling or state of being, occurs after about 20 minutes of continuous movement. It takes a while for the body to catch up to the mind. Continuous movement allows the body's "mood" to absorb the intent to exercise. Forcing the body to act before it is ready to agree with the mind produces the opposite effect – a harsh feeling of stress. Many people unfortunately mistake this feeling as being necessary for a worthwhile workout.

So that running does not become an additional source of stress, it is important to approach it properly. Come at it with a sense of exploration. Look upon running as an adventure in self-therapy leading to self-knowledge. Approach the minutes of your workout with the idea of keeping them as a comfortable interlude in your hectic day. As you get into your jogging shoes, leave the harried concerns of your daily life while you go to find how your body reacts to the run. Win or lose, pass or fail, impress or flop – all of these are totally irrelevant to the present moment. Running is something that you can do for yourself without strain or stress. Just enjoy it. Have the patience to preserve some minutes three or more times a week and generate the renewable discovery that regular running yields more personal gains than you ever imagined.

Soon you will experience a profound insight: stressful feelings and aerobic running are enemies. Indulging in one cancels the other. Comfortable running slowly dissipates internal stress. Regular running is an easy, non- competitive way that also leaves the runner in a balanced mood which may last for hours after the workout and carries over into his daily life.

Running Improves Health

The physical benefits of running are obvious to those who run: muscles are toned up, complexion becomes clear and rosy, the resting heart rate slows and becomes more efficient, excess weight is reduced. Medical research also is reporting more and more on the increased health of people who exercise, particularly those who run.

The fifth annual report on the health status of the nation from the United States Department of Health and Human Services lists more widespread physical activity as one of the factors explaining the declining heart disease mortality rate. From the *New England Journal of Medicine* one learns that regular exercise, such as running, improves one's ability to use oxygen, thus aiding those who suffer from diabetes.

A six-week study of six untrained, healthy adults showed that regular exercise (in this case four one-hour workouts) vastly improved their ability to utilize insulin in the body. Dr. V. R. Romon and four associates from the Yale School of Medicine who conducted this investigation concluded that the "increase in insulin sensitivity correlated directly with the improvement in physical fitness."

In studies of blood chemistry, running is shown to produce an unexpected benefit. The levels of the protein HDL (high-density lipoprotein) are higher and the concentration of LDL (low-density lipoprotein) is lower. In other words, the clogging or the narrowing of arteries is lessened by the improvement of the blood composition. Even though research has not fully explained why an exercise like running promotes this effect, it nevertheless seems to occur even when the runner stays on a diet rich in fat. In addition, running stimulates the process whereby blood clots are dissolved.

According to the *American Medical Joggers Association Newsletter* of 1981, there is work being done on the relationship of running and cancer. Presbyterian St. Luke's Medical Center in Denver, Colorado, has a self-help program for cancer patients which encourages exercise, running included. This program is based on the research of cancer specialists, such as Dr. Carl Simonton and Dr. Paul Hamilton, and shows evidence that cancer may be a psychosomatic disease. Thus, the mental state of the patient, especially depression and emotional stress, impairs the immunological systems of the body. When this happens, the body can not fight abnormal cell production. In the self-help program, patients run to reduce stress levels in themselves, thus permitting the cancer to go into a state of remission.

In 1971, Dr. Paul Jerustrom was almost bed-ridden by hepatic cirrhosis of the liver and ruptured esophageal vessels. Recuperation was agonizingly slow. His stamina barely lasted half a day, with rest filling the remaining hours. After living six months with the possibility of reoccurrence at any time, he had an idea. As a physician and pathologist, he knew that the repair of the body requires oxygen; why couldn't the regenerative capacity of the body's organs be enhanced by increased supplies of oxygen? Instead of resting, he began to take walks. Eventually, these brief excursions extended to an hour of brisk walking each day. Finally, he added jogging to the program. In 1978 Dr. Jerustrom ran the Boston Marathon in 3 hours, 1 minute. He was 57 years old.

In southern California, members of SCOR (Specialized Coronary Outpatient Rehabilitation Jogging Club) have helped cardiac patients, or those prone to heart disease, to develop individualized running programs. One 45-year-old man endured a heart attack with occlusion in the three major coronary arteries. Six years later he was running his way to 30 marathons in 17 months. When another 70-year-old member began feeling chest pains, an angiogram revealed 90 to 100% occlusion in his three major coronary arteries. Three years later he also completed his first marathon. Another member improved himself after three cardiac bypass operations to the point where he also completed a marathon successfully.

The positive evidence for people in poor debilitated health being able to recover and improve their state of well-being is accumulating. From around the country and from other parts of the world, clinical data as well as personal testimonials indicate that intelligent running builds mental and physical strength to cope with the various impedences to health that each person has acquired.

Running does not necessarily reverse the damage acquired by a life style of abusive living, but slow, long-distance running protects against many serious diseases. Even where hereditary factors may precipitate problems, running can improve the cardiovascular operation to the point where weakness may be minimized. Running can stimulate the potentials for both prevention and recovery. There are even instances where consistent exercise has enabled the body to forge natural bypasses to compensate for narrowed arteries. As runner cardiologist Dr. George Sheehan points out, "Whatever diseases you have will be improved by running."

Running is Fun

Play, like love, ranks as one of the highest of human potentials. It is important because the value of life needs protection from the humdrum, the over scheduling and list-making that occupies so much of our energies. We divide our day into ends and means, and forget that life does not always work by business rules. Life has moments which are too profound for measuring by production schedules or computerized statistics. Life is more than a time clock. Within life there are artful activities that allow us to catch up with ourselves. Running is one of them.

Play and sport have a certain innate appeal. An underlying presupposition in running for fitness is that running should always involve a degree of ease and playfulness. Once you forget that essential, you are doomed to repeat the stressful mistakes of all those tension-filled people who reduce their running to harsh schedules, or follow an ethical proposition that Stoic philosophers would have been proud of: the more it hurts, the better it is for me. People can run well without it becoming a dreadful experience.

When it comes right down to it, most people will continue to run only because they enjoy it. Their original motivation – health, competition, envy – may have impressed their family physician or spouse but it won't last on that basis alone. It is to go out and perspire in an activity that had no tangible recompense if they did not enjoy it.

Running makes people amateurs in the highest sense of that word. "Amateur" means "lover," and no one can love for long that which is not enjoyable. In running, people discover their delayed potential whose realization brings a sense of personal fulfillment. It is this rediscovered sense of doing and enjoying a free human act that sustains the runner.

Running also reawakens older, valuable memories of those years when being outdoors in the air and sunshine wooed us to nature and the uninhibited movements of our bodies. We left this enriching experience behind because we thought growing up meant growing beyond them. As youth fades, we accept the middle-aged change of life with some trepidation. Must we surrender to the rumor of middle age and turn it into the superstition of aging? Not if we take up running.

Running can become one of those changes of life that relink us to the memory of a forgotten time, not for reminiscence's sake, but for retrieving the power of fun and exploring it anew as a maturing adult.

Running Coordinates Mind and Body

Running is not meditation. Some writers attempt to promote it on that basis, without understanding the full process of mediation. Nonetheless, there are periods during the run when one experiences a sense of coordinated tranquility. Running then feels virtually effortless, as though one could continue forever. To some extent, this sort of experience repeats itself in varying degrees from time to time. Research has shown that when the limbic system of the brain is sufficiently stimulated by breathing, there is an increase in the release of gland secretions or endorphins. The presence of these secretions, pervading the body through the blood stream, has a tranquilizing effect on the body, thus minimizing the feeling of discomfort. This state of pleasurable activity is sometimes confused with a familiar state of inactivity experienced during meditation.

Running, however, does promote concentration. The notion of concentration is not meant to conjure up stern faces, grimacing with every step. That draining approach only incites the problems of tension. The concentration meant here presumes the relaxation that allows for the coordination of the mind and body.

The body takes its lead from the mind. If the mind is a thousand miles away while the body is undergoing a task, then there is separation, rather than coordination of the human being. Distracting your mind from the body's activities impedes performance and reduces enjoyment. One soon forfeits the experience of rhythmic coordination, and the resulting loss of bodily awareness invites injury. It is easy to strain the body when one does not listen to it.

The runner, on the contrary, should sustain attention upon easy, slow movement of the body. When the rhythm of breathing, the arm and leg motion, and the sounds of the steps are gracefully engaged, then the awareness of the passing environment adds to the session.

In a way, the performance of sport and play demonstrates the ancient discipline of yoga, which means union. The moment you coordinate mind and body, unifying your entire person with the activity, you have fulfilled the conditions for experiencing yoga. Running should be performed as a unified activity. Cultivate relaxed concentration. Listen to your body. Hear what it is telling you about pleasure and discomfort, heartbeat, and breathing, when to slow down and when to stop. You are an artist at serious play, personally integrating all the aspects of your body and mind, creating a new awareness of yourself in motion.

The Goal of Enduring Fitness

Right now you have achieved a certain degree of fitness. Your age, sex, work experience, and cultural background have gone into forming your present state of fitness. While everyone is different, few of us can say that an improvement of our state is impossible. The cultural atmosphere surrounding the new century has encouraged a wave of interest in health and endurance. But people don't improve their fitness by the occasional haphazard workout; jogging once in a while has little effect in establishing endurance. For lasting improvement one needs to consider running as part of one's lifestyle. One ought to run every day, or at least three or four times a week. If this running is carried out intelligently, that is, respecting the level of condition one starts from and the level one wants to achieve, then daily running becomes a new experience in healthful self-discovery.

Lifetime fitness can become your legacy. Every bit of the program here has that in mind, with the assurances that the end result will be gradually internalized. Thus, with continual running one comes to understand every aspect of running: warming up, walking, stretching, cooling down, diet, physiology.

The experience of enduring fitness, then, unifies and measures all the activities performed towards its achievement. This goal presents itself as a lifetime achievement. In itself, however, it is not the goal of life, but an outstanding presupposition for just about anything one attempts.

By now you have read enough to note that the philosophy of running espoused in this book is that your running moments should be gratifying and not debilitating. Forcing them to descend into a compulsive routine only robs your potential for lifelong restoration. Resist overpowering your body by depleting your reserves through harsh running. Be consistent, but take it easy. Arrange your workouts as an expression of your personal interest in the development of enduring fitness. The power and satisfaction of running lay dormant. Like any acquired art, you need patience in arousing these potentials. When you show concern, running becomes a source of renewal and a revelation of the magic of your life.

2

Internal Dynamics of Running

Running is a voluntary act of self-motion requiring coordination and compensatory adjustments in the entire body. The human body is so marvelously evolved that running has become an extremely efficient and natural consequence of its structure. A trained human being can outrun any animal in long distances. The release of movement through walking and running can be vastly improved as well. Even the most awkward beginners can, with patience, transform their inefficient movements into a relaxed, graceful style that produces a display of fluid beauty. It is merely a matter of attentive practice.

Agility of movement demands the efficient coordination of the entire body. Development of running skills relies upon the execution of metabolic functions in conjunction with nervous, muscular, skeletal, circulatory, and respiratory systems.

A human's legs house the strongest bones and muscles in the

body, making up about half of the body weight. Running is only possible when the leg muscles contract and relax. Their length must be shortened, thus pulling the bones to which they are attached into movement. The contraction is then released, so that the motion can expand in the opposite direction. We see this in the forward motion of walking, as the legs move alternately forward and backward. The flow of motion happens so naturally that one rarely reflects upon the dynamics of its achievement. In running, the muscles act in teams.

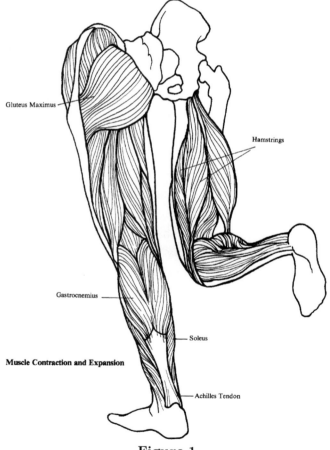

Figure 1

Movement requires that certain muscles act in concert with each other on opposite sides of their common joint. Movement results from the continual antagonistic interplay between muscles in their connection to their joints. Running is very different from hopping or skipping; the motion of the legs requires that each leg move in opposite direction to the other (see figure 1).

The intent of running is generated in the nervous system which then controls the alternate contraction and relaxation of the leg muscles. The microscopic muscle fibers undergo a series of muscle twitches that initiate the movement. As the activity intensifies, the heartbeat increases, the lungs expand and contract rapidly, and the oxygen and glucose-laden blood fuels the action of the muscles.

When one begins to run, the mind exerts a monitoring influence over the force of contraction. While the muscles always undergo contraction and relaxation in an automatic sequence, their speed is regulated by the runner's intention. The mind sets the pace. One runs, within one's own condition, faster or slower as wished. Except for sprinting, which should not be done unless one is thoroughly conditioned, running does not require use of muscles at their full strength.

To prevent injury one should pay attention to the way the legs feel during running. There is a constant feedback to the mind of the entire experience of running. The mind can then make alternating adjustments in the pace according to how the body responds to the pace. These adjustments depend upon the runner's intent as well as on the strength of the skeletal muscles involved. When someone starts running regularly, the contractile power of his legs may increase by 50% in less than a month. With steady, but not obsessive practice, running builds strength and endurance.

When the beginner's present state of muscle strength is challenged during prolonged effort, the body improves the functioning of the internal organs as well as the efficiency of movement of the arms and legs. One feels more comfortable about the daily practice. The early stiffness or muscle soreness recedes as the muscle improves its capacity for prolonged exercise. There are gains in flexibility and endurance. The unused physical potentials are being utilized.

Some people may feel that they are so out of condition or have abused their body for so long that a program of running is out of the question for them. A simple misunderstanding is involved here, and it can be quite costly, in preventing one from reaping decades of better health. Too often we imagine barriers to our well being when there is no evidence to justify our hesitation. Not long ago, Harold Chapson of California decided to exercise. He had run in college, but after he settled into his career, he had 44 years of a very sedentary existence. He began to run. Three years of running led him into his first Masters race. He set a world record for his age category. He was then 70 years old, nearly the life expectancy of American men. He has continued to run and improve each year since.

Being out of shape is not an incurable condition. It is just a matter of being consistent, yet flexible, in the workout. Being punctual on the designated practice days stimulates the body into its new adjustments for improving itself. With regular practice the body gradually accepts the runner's intent and responds by making profound adjustments.

When one is involved in casual walking or is at rest, the utilization of energy is minimal. To start running, even slowly, places a sudden new demand upon the body to cope with the exercise. It takes some seconds for the body to adjust processing the oxygen to fit the increased demands now put upon it. A temporary condition of oxygen shortage ensues. Sometimes one may feel a mild stress as he begins to run, until the body adjusts to the pace. Sometimes one may feel a little out of breath, but as the body settles into an easy pace, the discomfort lessens. What has taken place is a diminution of the momentary buildup of lactic acid during the run. The oxygen shortage reverses itself. Lactic acid recedes. The body warms up from the movement.

The internal adjustments are now stimulated into readiness to absorb and process the oxygen in a faster, more efficient manner.

Running uses energy. Research generally indicates that the immediate energy required for running is attributed specifically to the presence of a special compound known as ATP (adenosine triphosphate). ATP resides within the muscle tissues and cells in limited, minute amounts when the body is at rest. It is also formed primarily within the muscles themselves—the mitochondria portion of the cell, to be exact. Running liberates the energy needed for leg movement. Consequently, when one starts running, the utilization of ATP needs constant replenishment. Without this continual resynthesis of ATP muscle fatigue would set in rapidly and very shortly bring the legs to a halt. The indispensable ingredients supplying the resynthesis are foodstuffs and oxygen. Running continues as long as these energy resources are plentiful within the body.

When the inspired oxygen is dissolved in the blood, it attaches itself to the protein in the red blood cells called hemoglobin. It is then transported to the muscle cells. Here a vital conversion takes place. The latent energy of the food consumed now oxidizes with the newly arrived oxygen. The food has been slowly digested until part of it is in the form of glucose. The net result of the combination of glucose and oxygen is the formation of ATP, carbon dioxide, water, and heat. The chemical formula looks like this:

$$C_6 H_{12} O_6 + 6 O_2 = 6 CO_2 + 6 H_2 O + \text{heat} + \text{energy}$$

The concrete illustration of this formula is experienced by the runner as she or he moves (work), feels warmer (heat), sweats (water), inhales (oxygen), and exhales (carbon dioxide). The cyclic process of energy production and expenditure is more complicated than the bare description above, but the point is that the energy for running is facilitated when there is enough oxygen available to supply the muscles at

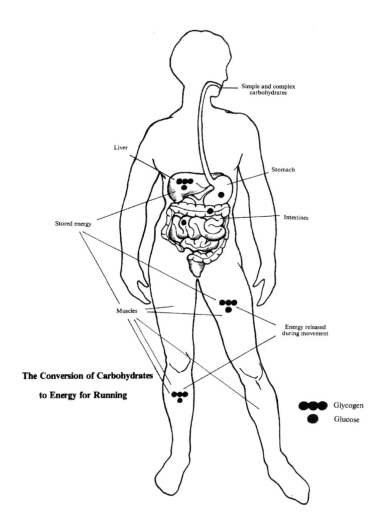

Simple and complex
carbohydrates

Liver

Stomach

Intestines

Stored energy

Muscles

Energy released
during movement

The Conversion of Carbohydrates

to Energy for Running

●●● Glycogen

● Glucose

Figure 2

the rate at which they are using it.

With continual running the reserves of ATP within the cells
would become depleted within a few seconds. Here is where the body's

dependence upon food enters the picture. The derivatives of food—carbohydrates, fats, and proteins—supply the cells with the necessary elements that contribute to the constant formulation of ATP during the day and when one is running. With the additional factor of oxygen in sufficient amount, the entire process, called the energy cycle, proceeds without a hitch. The conversion of foodstuffs and especially the supply of oxygen are the two essential factors needed for the production of energy for running.

The Anaerobic State

What happens when you are running so far or so hard that your legs start to feel heavy, your breath becomes labored, and a muscular tenseness expands across the entire body? This condition of intense fatigue indicates more often than not that oxygen is being insufficiently supplied to the muscles. Although running is becoming more and more painful, you can still run to some extent. But the harder you try to keep going, the more your tense legs move more and more slowly. It is no longer a case of mind over matter, but just the reverse.

The mind says run, but the body cannot do it because of the diminishing amounts of oxygen. You are rapidly reaching the point where running will come to a standstill. You are literally running out of breath. Physiologically, this cessation of movement corresponds to the lessening of the presence of oxygen to make ATP. The demand for energy is now greater than the body's ability to supply oxygen to produce it. Without adequate oxygen, a different chemical reaction takes place. Another inhibiting substance emerges and diffuses itself into the blood and muscles. It is lactic acid. The growing presence of lactic acid in place of oxygen means that less and less energy can be produced. This powerful acid inhibits the further production of ATP, and thus induces the tense feeling of "being tired." The body has been brought to the painful state where the expenditure of energy now exceeds the supply of oxygen. As we try to run faster or farther, leg movement becomes harder and stiffer. The feelings of pain increase. The chest, neck, arms, shoulders, and leg muscles begin to tighten more and more as lactic acid constricts their movement. As the heart vainly tries, as fast as it can, to supply the oxygen, we become more breathless. We need to rest. Our muscles are starving for oxygen.

We have run to the deficient point, where we are suffering from what is known as an "oxygen debt." We are breathing as fast as we can and still cannot get enough oxygen to the muscles in order for them to perform their work. We must reverse the process in some way in order to restore the balance between breathing and running if we are to continue to run. We may have the will to continue, in spite of the pain, but the fatigued stage will nevertheless prevent the muscles from continuing farther. We are running anaerobically.

The ability to run comfortable can be restored in one of two ways. First, we can stop running and allow the body to recover its breathing equilibrium by walking. Or, second, we can slow down the running pace until it is comfortable and then interject walking. In either case we are allowing for the supply of oxygen to restore itself to a proper balance. We are "catching up" with our breath. We are reducing the constrictive presence of lactic acid in the muscles. More than anything else, muscular fatigue is due to this overabundance of lactic acid, which is formed principally when we are unable to absorb sufficient oxygen quickly enough to get the energy we need.

Achieving the Steady Rhythmic Breath State

How can we increase the absorption of oxygen? The answer is actually very simple:

- Run in a way that expands the capacity to absorb oxygen and prevents oxygen debt.
- Run in a steady, rhythmic, breathful state.

That's the secret. The exercise of running with rhythmic breathing is ironic, in that it uses up oxygen while simultaneously increasing the body's capacity to absorb and use oxygen, thus warding off fatigue. Unlike a machine, the human body does not wear out primarily through use. A machine cannot supply its own substance for existence, but the body improves its ability to perform by performing.

By using the very substances that it requires—glycogen and oxygen— in order to exist and to do its task of running, the body upgrades its ability to process them. The body should never be compared to a machine in performance. The body is a living, organic, growth-oriented substance, and running is a vital activity which enhances the total being of the body, fostering higher performance.

Increased level of performance shows in ease of movement and progressive improvements in endurance. Regulated action improves endurance. The promotion of endurance forestalls fatigue, which is another way of saying that the generation of lactic acid is minimal when one is running in a steady breath state.

The most efficient means of achieving efficient performance is to run in such a way that oxygen is supplied as needed for the pace of the running. This experience is the steady breath state. However, there is a gradation here, depending upon the condition of the runner. For some, an 18-minute mile pace achieves this steady state level. For others, it could be a 12- or 6 1/2-minute per mile pace. Consistent running or training makes the difference, along with age and body weight. Speed is not what counts. What is crucial is the development of a rhythmic breath pattern which allows one to run "with oxygen," to run aerobically.

Running in a steady, rhythmic breath cycle involves widespread physiological adjustments. While one is primarily using the heart, lungs and legs, the entire body gradually undergoes a physical reorganization. Even though other muscular regions and organs are not directly responsible for the expenditure of energy in running, they nevertheless participate in support and are, in turn, enriched by the new activity.

For example, the cardiovascular system and the respiratory system are greatly benefited. Running stimulates the growth of mitochondria, those production sites of ATP, and increases the reserve glycogen, the storage of the foodstuffs in the liver and running muscles. These organic improvements permit quicker elimination of waste products from muscular metabolism. A major overhaul within the body has now effected a healthier status for the runner's resting condition, as well as for the running.

Effects of Running on Leg Muscles

Aerobic long-distance running results in elevated glycogen stores in the muscles and more vascularity around individual muscle fibers. When muscles begin to tire, there is a gradual accumulation of acid waste products, the residue from the thousands of sequential contractions of the leg muscles. The net movement of fluids occurring during circulation of the blood becomes insufficient to prevent the formation of an acid condition in the muscles. Waste products are then not carried into the bloodstream at the rate they are produced; fatigue then follows.

Some days when you are feeling full of the desire to run, you may overextend yourself to the point where the effects remain unnoticeable until hours afterwards. Then, sore muscles! Your calf feels stiff when you walk or tender when you squeeze it. A mild buildup of waste products occurs that cannot be removed completely during the running time. These products of muscle metabolism, including excessive fluids at the muscle site, make the muscle temporarily shorter and thus resistant to stretching. When we get up the next morning we find this stiffness or mild tension in our legs when we walk. Painful as the muscles feel, their further use during the day in ordinary walking and climbing stairs actually aids their recovery. The increased circulation provided by the leg movement disperses the wastes and allows the swelling to be reabsorbed. Rest merely prolongs the soreness, while mild exercise and massage rehabilitate the legs faster.

Constant physical activity effects new adaptations by the muscles. Exercising them increases their capacity for more exercise. At the same time, one acquires a certain immunity against soreness. This phenomenon of adaptability may be found at all ages.

The current level of endurance can be extended with regular workouts. In fact, the body adapts and thrives on regular exercise. It increases its resistance to earlier levels of tiredness. What seemed tiring some weeks ago, now comes with ease. The exertion of gentle, rhythmic breathing with running upsets the sedentary balance of the body's internal environment. When running is sustained for a quarter of an hour or more, the inner regulating systems of the body are profoundly stimulated into reestablishing their balance, but not at their former restrictive level. A wondrous biological transformation occurs. While the body recovers its normal state of balance—homeostasis— after the workout, it is not at the previous level of operation. The internal environment reintegrates at a higher level of operation. An upgraded—allostasis state—balance occurs. Running and vigorous walking constantly challenges the conditioning of the body. One's fatigue threshold is pushed back. Consequently, both health and running performances are progressively enhanced, and even the resting state of the runner is improved.

The improvement in strength and endurance, however, does not make bulky legs. The muscle contours do improve, with each muscle gradually becoming more clearly defined on the surface of the body, but enlargement of skeletal muscles beyond their normal size (hypertrophy) results only from intensive overloading and using exercises done by sprinters and weightlifters. Running tends to trim excessive fat from the body, especially from those regions involved in performing the exercise itself. When the muscles are exercised in this way, flabbiness vanishes.

Endurance running stimulates the reconstitution of tissue into more red fibers, augmenting the concentration of myoglobin. The oxygen requirement for distance running causes the body to develop these slow oxidative skeletal muscle fibers. This increase is in contrast with the production of white fibers associated with weight training and similar power activities, which thicken the fibers and enlarge the muscle, but fatigue rapidly. Actually, distance runners possess both types of muscle fibers. The predominance of red fibers means that oxygen reaches the muscle fibers more easily, thus improving endurance. The presence of white fibers aids the runner in fast energy utilization, such as sprinting. While continuous distance running produces very restricted gains in muscle enlargement, the growth of red fibers complements the upgrading of the oxygen transport and its utilization in the muscles.

Collateral Circulation Augmented

Steady, long running with rhythmic breathing places a modest load upon the dynamics of energy metabolism which increases the vascularity of the muscles so that they can accept a larger blood flow. Since new capillaries form, and unused ones reopen, the muscle fibers receive the nourishment needed to compensate their improved endurance. Even the myoglobin which shunts the oxygen from the hemoglobin to the mitochondria is now in denser supply, along with the latter factors. The delivery of blood throughout the body is vastly more efficient than for the sedentary person.

Prolonged running also increases the perfusion of blood in skeletal muscles. The body diverts more blood from less active tissues to the active muscles. Blood vessels dilate in the muscles, but constrict in the abdominal organs and inactive muscles. (That's a good reason for not running on a full stomach or shortly after eating.) The heart fills and squeezes more efficiently, the velocity of the blood quickens to the cells, and the lungs ventilate more effectively.

The ability to improve endurance for long runs may also be associated with the increased production of the body's internal opiates. Endorphins, as they are called, are the natural endogenous pain relievers generated at least within the limbic systems of the brain. After about 20 minutes of steady running, the amount of endorphins within the runner's blood levels increases, producing a kind of anesthesia against pain and, in abundance, what is described as a feeling of euphoria. It is quite possible that since the limbic system is immediately stimulated through the nerve endings in the roof of the nasal cavity, breathing through the nostrils may be the catalyst that inspires their increased secretion.

These unique biological improvements are some of the remarkable ways in which the organs and systems of the body react to an intelligent program of running. It is not surprising, then, that one day the runner will be able to complete 1, 6, 10 or more miles at an even pace in a quiet, normal breathing state without seeing life flash before him or her at the finish.

3

The Breath of Life

If we were to single out the most crucial factor in successful running, we would say "breathing." How one breathes determines the beneficial development or the eventual abuse of one's heart, lungs, nervous system, and physical prowess. Breathing is the dynamic expression of the human respiratory system. The composition of the body involves the intricate placement and coordination of many other systems: glandular, cardiovascular, excretory, and so forth, but all of these systems take their cue from the way one breathes. Strange as it may seem, the respiratory system, seen from the aspect of breathing, is the major influence upon the entire metabolism of the body. The heart cannot pump without breath, digestion and cell repair cannot proceed without breath, and the brain and its glandular secretions are unable to function without breath. Nothing vital happens in the body without its dependence in some way upon breathing. One can refuse to eat or drink or sleep for a day, but how long can he tolerate the lack of breath? We can say that breathing is the very foundation of health.

The importance of proper breathing is normally overlooked. The average person does not give breathing a second thought; one's breathing just goes on. Why should one be concerned with something that occurs so effortlessly and automatically? The fact that breathing continues with relative ease and without calling attention to itself does not imply that one's breathing is functioning for optimum health. In most cases the opposite is true.

The average adult breathes about 23,000 to 26,000 times in a day, that is, about 16 to 18 times a minute. When one gets angry or excited, the breath rate increases in a strained fashion. Likewise, when one feels sad or despondent, the breath rate decreases irregularly. During the day, breathing proceeds in a very uneven manner, often related to the events of the surrounding environment. When one takes up vigorous exercise, the breath rate increases with such rapidity and force that one feels the change throughout the entire body. The more one is unconditioned for the demands of exercise, the greater the effort put forth in breathing. The less one uses the lungs fully, the weaker their condition becomes, affecting the entire metabolism adversely. The strength of breathing relates to everything that one thinks or does. It is truly the barometer of life.

Proper breathing has become a lost art. By not taking it seriously, people lose its potential benefits, and runners are no exception. In their workouts runners approach breathing like starved exiles coming upon a banquet. They breathe as fast as they can during running, using both nose and mouth. Although competitive runners want abundant air, they are forced by their harsh and driving approach to use oxygen as much and as quickly as possible. "If they could get additional air," Dr. Joan Ullyat remarked to me, "they would breathe through their ears!"

The question is: does running well require such furious breathing? Can one achieve superb fitness without exposing the lungs and heart to such Herculean demands? Can one improve speed and stamina without violent, harsh breathing? In a word, the answer is "yes."

Breathing in a regulated manner, sustaining a rhythmic flow of inspiration and expiration, can achieve amazing results in runners who will have the patience to develop their training or workouts according to a coordinated breath pattern. For people who desire to enjoy their running and to promote a high state of fitness, developing these goals around their breathing can bring utterly satisfying results without abuse to their internal systems. Dr. Kenneth Cooper of the famous Aerobics Institute in Dallas, Texas, insists that "the key to endurance training is oxygen consumption."

For several years I have involved myself in some careful experimentation with breathing techniques for running. These techniques are based upon an accurate understanding of the physiology and kinesthesiology of the internal systems activated by running. Building upon observation of the natural process of breath at various phases of its operation, including sedentary breathing, walking, steep climbing and running at various speeds, it has become quite evident to me, as well as to those I have trained in this method, that the dynamics of breath can become the foundation for a successful running program.

The adjustment to this breath program is not a complex matter, but at the same time it cannot occur overnight. People have established breathing habits. Once these are fostered, the results speak for themselves. In order to see how these breathing techniques operate, it is important to understand the structure and the coordinated dynamics of the respiratory system.

Structure of the Lungs

The chest houses the remarkable lungs, the essential organs of respiration. These two spongy masses of tissue extend from just above the clavicle down to their floor, the diaphragm (see Figure 3). Together, on either side of the heart, they fill out the width and height of the thoracic cavity. The cone shape of both lungs is wider in the lower half than at the apex. This broader convex segment retains a larger network of capillaries, which enables more oxygenated blood to pass through here than in the upper lobes; the shorter and broader right lung contains three lobes, while the left lung contains two lobes, with the heart nestling in its indented center.

The light, porous texture of the lungs is extremely elastic, hence their capacity for inflation and deflation. The structural connections that allow the air to enter the lungs from the mouth or nose resemble an upside-down tree. The trunk of the tree is the windpipe, or trachea, which extends from the larynx in the throat downward through the midcenter of the chest. The descending trachea branches out into the

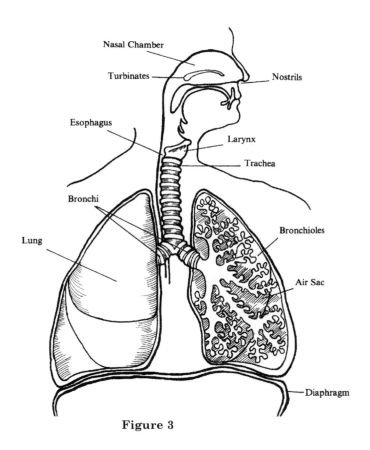

Figure 3

lungs, dividing into the bronchi, three for the right lobes and two for
the left lobes. These main bronchi divide again to smaller branches or
bronchioles, which sprout the leaves of the tree, the alveoli. It is these
terminal sites that produce the actual exchange between the air and
the blood.

The Running Instrument: The Nose

Most runners breathe through the mouth, taking advantage of
the larger opening in order to get the most possible air. Yet the nose is
the proper organ for breathing, even when running. The nose, along
with the connecting internal organs which lead to the windpipe, provide the proper passageway for the air to reach the lungs and for the
discharge of carbon dioxide. The double passageway, the nostrils, are
interiorly covered by a thick mucous membrane. The inner regions of
the nostrils serve many indispensable purposes.

First, the air rushing over the membrane does not go straight
down into the windpipe; rather, it curves around, due to the protrud-
ing surfaces, or turbinates. The air is swirled around to be warmed
and moistened before proceeding to fill the lungs, thus preventing
shock to the lungs when the outside air is cold or dry. The body can
thus be conditioned to run in very cold temperatures. Secondly, the
mucous membrane is coated with fine hairs or cilia, similar to those
found in the trachea. They filter polluted air in order to prevent irritating foreign particles from entering the lungs and causing infection.
If, by chance, some minute pollutants should escape detection by the
nasal passageways and the trachea, the alveoli are equipped with an
army of predatory organisms called macrophages. These white blood
cells tend to annihilate any foreign invaders in maintaining the respiratory's protective system.

The division of the nose into two nostrils focuses the breathing
during the day and night. Throughout the 24 hours, we vary in
breathing predominantly through the left or the right nostril. Most of

the time we are not aware of this oscillating fact. Yet we are very much aware of our transition in moods, which are affected by the changing breath cycle.

In a healthy adult, one nostril is predominant for approximately two hours before the flow of air is shifted to the other nostril, making it predominant. The reason we sometimes notice that it is harder to breathe through one nostril than the other is because the erectile tissue lining one nostril becomes swollen with blood, while the lining of the other nostril remains in a shrunken condition until the flow alters itself. This transition, or ultradian rhythm, as it is called, can be shortened or lengthened depending upon our internal and external responses to the events of the day.

The ease of breath flow, or nostril dominance, has been studied extensively over the centuries by yogis, who have noted the pertinent relationship between the breath flow and its impact upon the body and mind. According to these ancient investigators, the various activities of the body and the mental mood of the individual are related to nostril dominance and the depth and pattern of breathing. Ordinarily, when the breathing force of the air is stronger in the right nostril, the individual feels in an active mood. The converse holds equally true when the breathing force of air alters to the left nostril. When the left nostril predominates, one desires more passive activities.

Running tends to produce either of the following two breath dominances. Usually the right nostril flares open during the run, associating with the vigorous activity, and there are moments when both nostrils sustain the force of air simultaneously. This equalized condition, which is briefly achieved at intervals during the 24 hours of the day as the dominance alter from one side to the other, produces a calming effect upon the individual. Running does not produce left nostril breathing. Even when the left side may have been dominant at the beginning of the workout, the body quickly alters the breath flow to the right side or to the middle state.

The Oxygen Transport System

In order to appreciate the principle of centering running upon the breath, let us consider the operation of the respiratory system. The air one breathes normally enters through the nostrils or the mouth, descending through the windpipe into the far reaches of the alveoli. There the inflation and deflation of these tiny air sacs diffuse the new air into the bloodstream, exchanging it for the old air, to be transported rapidly throughout the body by the heart's incessant squeezing movements.

The squeezing of the heart sends the incoming venous blood into the pulmonary artery for oxygen rejuvenation. This blood is bluish red in color, since the body has exhausted its oxygen content. Simultaneously, during the same squeezing of the heart, rejuvenated blood at the site of the lungs hurries back to the heart and into the aorta in order to supply the body's capillaries with fresh fuel. This oxygenated blood is bright red due to the presence of iron in the blood cell. This cycle repeats itself thousands of time throughout the day, the bronchial tree servicing the body with ever-fresh air upon inspiration, and receiving from the venous blood the used portion of fuel (carbon dioxide) upon expiration.

The alveoli, numbering nearly 700 million, expand and contract with the air in the lungs. They permit the exchange of gases, trading off venous debris of waste carbon dioxide for fresh oxygen. The new air diffuses through the thin membrane walls of the alveoli and attaches to the waiting red blood cells within the capillaries; the contacting process occurs one cell at a time within the capillaries. Waiting within each red blood cell is a protein which attaches itself to the molecules of oxygen and carries off its vital treasure via the heart to the various parts of the body that need to be enlivened. On the return trip to the lungs via the heart, these same blood cells do not flow back to the lungs empty-handed. After depositing its oxygen, the hemoglobin combines with carbon dioxide, the residue gas from the working cells' release of energy, and streams back to the lungs, where it drops off the residue for exhalation and replenishes itself again.

This system of oxygen transport actually takes place in less than a second for each blood cell in its capillary holding dock. All the faster must this blood cycle proceed when one is running. The blood moves through the lungs and heart at the rate of four to six liters per minute while one is lying down; if one is sitting or standing up, the rate decreases slightly under the dragging pressure of gravity. But running enforces an enormous velocity upon the blood flow. Between 20-30 liters per minute circulate, depending upon the runner's condition.

The more a runner understands the factors permitting vigorous exercise, the more s/he can appreciate the functional interrelationship between the organs of the body. In a true sense, the lungs, heart, and blood vessels sustain the complete respiratory system.

Three Types of Breathing

Unlike the heart, the lungs are basically passive. They cannot depress or expand of their own accord. They are unable to absorb fresh air or expel stale air on their own; for this they need assistance. For their operation, these organs utilize the surrounding environment: the muscles alongside the ribcage, those of the abdominal region, and especially the diaphragm, that curved sheet of muscle separating the lungs and heart from the lower visceral organs. The combined pressure of these three areas against the lungs and their subsequent release stimulates the exchange of gases by the lungs.

Animals breathe by instinct; man breathes by instinct and volition. Animals cannot control their breathing; man can exert his will over the cadence of his breath cycle. The liberty which man processes in the expression of breathing enables him to achieve performances that are completely impossible for the animal kingdom. With volition, a man can direct his breathing in one of three different ways: chest breathing, clavicular breathing, and diaphragmatic breathing.

Chest breathing moves the air into the lungs by expanding the chest, or thorax. This occurs readily among runners as well as non-runners. Breathing with the emphasis upon expanding the chest fills the middle and upper portion of the lungs, while minimizing the lower lobes. The deliberate expansion of the chest invokes the activation of the intercostal muscles in between the ribs, which actually swing upward and forward, allowing a greater volume of air to inflate the lungs. The lifting of the ribcage requires more energy than any other type of breathing, and thus causes the heart to work harder.

Clavicular breathing is rarely employed except in emergencies when someone may be utterly exhausted or winded and needs maximum air. It is an excellent practice to start the day. By controlling the inhalation from the lower lobes to the top of the lungs, which rest near the clavicle bones, and back again, one can purify the lungs from the carbon dioxide built up during sleep. Obviously, it demands a great amount of energy to perform the entire process, and thus it is not the normal method of breathing.

Diaphragmatic breathing is the third type. The most efficient manner of breathing in virtually all circumstances, it employs the maximum use of the diaphragm. This unique muscle is the movable floor of the lungs. Most important, it can be directly influenced by the human will.

Proper ventilation occurs when the dome-shaped diaphragm relaxes upward, compressing the lungs for exhalation, and then tightens and flattens downward, allowing for the recoil of the lungs and the consequent entrance of fresh air into them. This reciprocal cycle is assisted throughout by the conjoined movement of the intercostal muscles of the ribcage, and specially the front of the abdominal wall. Although the lungs are squeezed and released from all sides, the emphasis remains upon the movement of the diaphragm.

There is an exercise which will help to develop diaphragmatic breathing and get one used to the feeling of correct breathing. Lie on your back with legs about a foot apart. Place your left hand on top of your chest and your right hand on the upper abdomen just at the edge of the ribcage. Relax completely and begin to pay attention to your breathing. Inhale slowly and deeply. As you inhale, you should feel the lower edge of the ribcage expand and the abdomen rise as the air fills the lungs. As you exhale you should feel your right hand lower as the muscles of the abdomen tighten to squeeze out the air. Think of a balloon filling with air and then flattening as the air is released. The left hand on your chest should not move at all. There is relatively no rise and fall of the chest when diaphragmatic breathing is done.

Diaphragmatic breathing is actually the most natural way to breathe. It is the way we breathe when we are unconscious, as in deep sleep. It is also the way a baby or a young child breathes before he has been told or affected otherwise. One can continue this beneficial practice during walking as well. When applied to running, there will be some raising of the upper chest as a natural extension of diaphragmatic breathing and the motion of the arms while running.

Breathing for Running

Running reflects your breathing style. How hard your heart has to work correlates with efficient breathing. Many runners impede their breathing and intensify their tiredness by mixing up the wrong muscles for breathing. They exert effort when they should relax and vice-versa. Runners illustrate this major fault by emphasizing forceful inhalation and being indifferent to the exhalation. This imbalance is probably a carryover from the faulty breathing most people demonstrate in their daily lives.

A mistake is made by assuming that one should raise and expand the upper chest and hold in the waist when the air is needed. This easily occurs when one is getting tired of loosing control of the breath. Puffing out the chest in order to get more air, however, jams the respiratory process. Emphasizing the chest enlarges the upper ribcage and flattens the abdominal wall against the diaphragm, forcing the ribcage and the diaphragm to work at odds. In this arrangement, one can only breathe partially at best, since the diaphragm can hardly descend. The constricted abdominal region and expanded ribcage producing the puffed chest keep the diaphragm locked upward, more or less unable to descend properly to allow the lungs a fuller refill.

It is like speeding up a car and at the same time applying the break. Consequently, this restricted breathing only increases the tense urgency of the air. The runner feels increased discomfort and tension as a result of high chest breathing.

Instead of deliberately lifting the chest during a run, one should emphasize the movement of the diaphragm in the contraction or exhalation phase of the breath cycle. Exercising the diaphragm allows for the richest exchange of the oxygenated blood, since most of the capillaries are in the lower portion of the lungs. As one gradually accustoms the nervous system to accept this constant movement, one will find that over a period of weeks the combined rhythm of the diaphragm with nasal breathing eliminates fatigue. When the runner gets into better condition and becomes accustomed to breathing diaphragmatically through the nostrils, the breathing rhythm can be further modified as explained in the chapter on the workout.

Running should build upon the natural, inborn disposition for diaphragmatic breathing. Just as brisk walking can be performed without strain by using the diaphragm with the air exchange passing through the nostrils, so running can be performed in the same manner. Sustaining the steady breath state can be gradually experienced as the foundation for enjoyable running without stress. A steady breath state insures the following advantages:

1) The experience of running produces less strain upon the body when one breathes diaphragmatically. The upper chest is not called into play; consequently the stimulation of the sympathetic nervous system is kept at a minimum. Neither oxygen consumption nor the

heart rate are excessive. Thus running requires less energy to perform and tiredness is forestalled.

2) Coordinated breathing lays the foundation for gradual improvements in endurance without wearing out the runner. Breathing smoothly through the nostrils sustains the runner's efforts, with the most comfortable impact upon the body. Accumulating strain is virtually impossible as long as oxygen is provided through steady, rhythmic breathing.

3) It is not long before the beginner can enjoy as much as an hour of continuous easy running. By interspersing creative pauses (slowing down the pace, doing stretches, walking slowly and briskly), the body can maintain and adjust its energy output over a long period without calling upon its reserves. Nervous energy is not brought to a state of near depletion, since one runs only as fast as the breathing rhythm allows. A sense of comfortable running is generated and kept intact throughout the period.

4) Hard running or fast running in a beginning runner produces a low concentration of oxygen and a high concentration of lactic acid and carbon dioxide, which in turn stimulates heavy or rapid breathing. Excessive amounts of carbon dioxide effect a quickening of the heart rate and the respiratory system. An unconditioned runner will soon begin gasping for air and feel increasing tension and fatigue due to lack of oxygen. By controlling one's pace through a steady breathing rhythm, one never incurs an oxygen imbalance while improving endurance.

5) Running "within the breath" allows the entire body to adjust itself to the increased demands put upon its various systems. This gradual adjustment includes the generation of hemoglobin which bears the oxygen to the body tissues. When we begin running in poor condition, there can be more oxygen fluctuating in our lungs than hemoglobin available to carry it to our leg muscles. Under normal sedentary conditions, the number of hemoglobin cells in circulation

remains stable. As old cells are destroyed every day, they are rapidly replaced by new ones, keeping the amounts relatively the same. Amazingly, under the stimulation of running, the body increases its production of hemoglobin cells, thus improving the oxygen-carrying system.

This enhanced process is comparable to taking up the sport of mountain climbing. At first, the higher you climb, the harder it is to breathe. After some weeks, however, a process of acclimatization sets in. The increased comfort indicates that the body has enlarged its supply of red blood cells in order to carry additional oxygen needed for the activity. Similarly, over a period of weeks, daily running stimulates the body's hemoglobin resources to enlarge its army, thus enriching the blood's capacity to absorb more oxygen from the lungs. The result? Breathing becomes easier, vitality improves, endurance grows.

Running at a steady breath state fosters a healthy condition in which the body's utilization of oxygen improves itself. When there is enough oxygen available for working the legs, one can run almost indefinitely – at least until the food stores are depleted or muscle soreness occurs. Rhythmic breathing that utilizes the diaphragm and nostrils allows for optimal metabolism during the workout. Since one is breathing most economically, there are no severe irregular strains interfering with the body's metabolism. The gradual promotion of endurance occurs over a period of weeks without the usual strains and pains of trying to coerce the body beyond its conditioned readiness.

The Oxygen Debt

A steady breathing state should be the norm for running. On the other hand, whenever the input of oxygen cannot keep up with the demands of the legs, an oxygen imbalance gradually takes place. Energy is still produced, but in a deficient manner which is costly for the runner. One is literally slowing down, suffering through an oxygen shortage. This condition is called anaerobic metabolism. Becoming breathless allows lactic acid and carbon dioxide to accumulate in the cells and flood the bloodstream. Running cannot thrive upon lactic acid. Its emergence indicates an oxygen debt; that is, the runner is using oxygen faster than he can replace it. When excessive carbon dioxide accumulates, it signals the brain to promote faster breathing. Now the breath rate and heartbeat rapidly increase as the internal systems strive mightily to supply the leg muscles with a short-term affair. The production of lactic acid spreads into the muscles of the body, nullifying their action. Energy production in now 19 times less than it was with an ample supply of oxygen. The runner begins to "tie up". Tiredness ensues. The fastest runner in the world could hardly last 300 meters under these conditions.

The runner has only two recourses: slow down or walk. In either option, the pressure of trying to run with decreasing amounts of oxygen is relieved. By allowing the breath pattern to restore its balance to a rhythmic interchange, the body can now rid itself of the wastes from the harsh running. There is no doubt that over a period of months, steady running enables the body to withstand even the strain of oxygen debt better than in an unconditioned state.

Occasional racing also improves this condition. However, the runner's goal of enjoyment through fitness does not require bouts with intense stress through oxygen debt. Progressive endurance can be achieved without submitting oneself to strenuous efforts that leave one breathless, irritable, and fatigued.

The Power in Breath

Breathing properly and eating nutritious food provides the body with the necessary energy to perform its tasks: yet the air we breathe and the nutrients we digest are not the primary source of our energy. According to the ancient investigators mentioned earlier, air and food are the grosser aspects of a fundamental energy that pervades the universe. This subtle life force that stimulates all vital activities, wherever these may be found, is referred to as *prana*. The Sanskrit word has its counterparts in other ancient traditions that study the energy systems of man and nature. The Japanese word ki and the Chinese word chi, for example, reflect the same meaning. The development of the martial arts of the East, as well as the physical and mental feats of the yogis, are founded upon an experiential understanding of the role of *prana*.

The power of pranic energy was aptly demonstrated in a study reported by Dr. James Funderburk in *Science Studies Yoga*. In 1967, Yogi Ramananda, a 106-pound Indian from Mysore, who had practiced pranic exercises for many years, used the power of *prana* for an unusual feat of strength. He was tested beforehand and showed the normal physical strength for his 67 years. Around his waist was wound a chain of 3/8th inch iron links. One end of the chain was measured at 650 pounds. Upon a given signal, Yogi Ramananda increased his breathing rate for one minute, inhaled for 13 seconds, and pressed his feet against the bar as he exhaled. The chain broke. The links did not bend apart; one link was completely severed.

In our modern investigation of human physiology we are cognizant of the chemical reactions and the physical activities of human behavior. Scientific scrutiny can discern even the molecular dispositions that comprise the various systems of human growth and action. Still, investigation has yet to uncover the subtlest foundation for human performance.

Prana, or the vital energy, is abundantly present in the air. The composition of the atmosphere serves as the vehicle or carrier of the *prana* for human assimilation. Breathing is the most important process for inspiring it. *Prana* disperses into the major electro-chemical activities that enable the person to exist and perform. Life and movement owe their existence to the continual presence of *prana*.

Running draws upon this life force in great quantities. The most efficient absorption of prana for vigorous exercise occurs when the principal organs for breathing execute their coordinated movements. The systematic use of diaphragmatic breathing in conjunction with the abdominal muscles and the nasal passageway ensures the optimum deployment of *pranic* energy.

The act of regulated breathing with running can correct the lack of vitality associated with defective breathing habits. Diaphragmatic nasal breathing slowly loosens and strengthens the muscular regions of the entire trunk area. The increased flexibility and coordination of the internal organs allows *prana* to increase its energizing presence throughout the entire body. This qualitative upgrading of vitality forms the corresponding basis of the improved oxygen transport system. Since one breathes deeper, more *prana* is vitalizing the cardiovascular system. The result? One's whole person feels more enlivened to go about life's duties.

To cleanse the respiratory system and to allow for better utilization of oxygen, yogis developed various breathing practices centuries ago. I have found the following to be very beneficial for runners, as they expand the lung capacity.

Alternate Nostril Breathing —*Nadi Shodhanam*

This breathing practice is excellent for balancing the nerve currents in the body, the active and passive, right and left sides of the body. Its basis is diaphragmatic breathing.

1) Sit comfortable with the head, neck, and trunk erect and relaxed. Close the mouth.

2) Bring your hand up to your nose and fold down the index finger and the middle finger so that the thumb and ring finger can be used to close the right and left nostrils.

3) With the thumb, gently close off the right nostril. Exhale gently and completely through the left nostril.

4) Immediately close off the left nostril with the ring finger and inhale slowly and completely through the right nostril. Inhalation and

exhalation should be approximately even.

5) Immediately close off the right nostril and exhale slowly and completely through the left nostril.

6) Close off the left nostril and inhale completely through the right nostril.

7) Close off the right nostril and exhale slowly and completely through the left nostril.

8) Close off the left nostril and inhale through the right nostril. Keep the left nostril closed and now exhale through the right nostril.

9) Close off the right nostril and inhale completely through the left nostril.

10) Repeat the exhalation through the right nostril and the inhalation though the left nostril twice more.

11) Place your hands on your lap and exhale and inhale completely through both nostrils three times. Here is a summary of the steps:

Exhale Left

Inhale Right

Exhale Left

Inhale Right

Exhale Left

Inhale Right

Exhale Right

Inhale Left

Exhale Right

Inhale Left

Exhale Right

Inhale Left

In the evening, begin by closing off the left nostril and exhaling from the right nostril. There should be no pause between the exhalation and inhalation. Breathing should be controlled, diaphragmatic, soundless, and without exertion. Three of the above cycles may be practiced at each sitting.

Kapalabhati Breathing

Kapalabhati, or breathing which "makes the forehead shine" cleans and invigorates the sinuses and the respiratory tract, as well as aids digestion.
1) Sit with the head, neck and trunk straight and erect.
2) Using the diaphragm and the abdominal muscles, forcefully and quickly expel all the breath.
3) Relax the abdominal muscles and allow a slow, easy, passive inhalation of breath.
4) Repeat the forceful expulsion and easy inhalation in quick succession 6 more times.
5) With practice, the cycles of exhalation and inhalation may be increased to 21.

Bellows —*Bhastrika*

In this breathing practice the abdominal muscles force the air in and out of the lungs like the working of a bellows. Like *kapalabhati,* bellows (*bhastrika*) cleans the respiratory tract of stale air and invigorates the system.
1) Sit with the head, neck, and trunk in a straight line.
2) Using the diaphragm and the abdominal muscles, forcefully and quickly expel all the breath.
3) Forcefully push out the abdominal muscles quickly and breathe in deeply and forcefully.
4) Continue to repeat the forceful inhalation and exhalation 6 more times.
5) With practice, the cycles of inhalation and exhalation may be increased to 21 times.

Sitali **Breathing**

This exercise as well as the following one is especially helpful for cooling and soothing the body on a hot day.

1) Sit erect with the head, neck and trunk erect.
2) Curl the tongue lengthwise so that it resembles a tube and let the tip of the tongue protrude outside the lips.
3) With a hissing sound, inhale through the mouth.
4) Exhale the breath completely through both nostrils.
5) Repeat 2 more times.

Sitkari **Breathing**

Like *sitali, sitkari* breathing also cools and soothes .

1) Sit erect with the head, neck, and trunk erect.
2) Roll the tongue back toward the soft palate.
3) Part the lips, clench the teeth and inhale air through the teeth, making a hissing sound.
4) Exhale completely through both nostrils.
5) Repeat 2 more times.

Nasal Wash

During the course of a day the nasal passages may collect mucus, sometimes dried or caked. This obstructs the passages to the sinuses and may cause sinus problems or headaches. The nasal wash is designed to eliminate these problems and soothe the nasal linings.

1) Select a small *neti* pot or cup with a spout and fill it with luke-warm water. Dissolve salt in the water so that the solution tastes like tears (about 1/4-1/2 teaspoon).

2) Bend forward over a sink, tilt your head to the left and pour the solution through the right nostril. Keep the mouth slightly open to breathe and allow the water to flow out the left nostril. You may need to make adjustments with the head position, in order to assure the

smooth flow of water.

3) Tilt the head to the right, pour the solution through the left nostril, and allow the water to flow out of the right nostril.

4) Blow through both nostrils simultaneously into the sink to clear the nose of excess water and mucus. Bend forward a few times to draw excess water from the nostrils.

4
The Heart
of the Matter

The heart is a strangely fascination organ. Basically it is a hollow muscle, in tissue composition quite unlike any other of the more that six hundred muscles in the body. It is functionally the most durable muscle of the body, for it never completely rests. It is made for endurance. It is the Rolls Royce of human organs.

A healthy heart's performance can be improved at any age. Runners who began a program of running at 60, 70, and 80 years of age, after leading rather sedentary careers, have become marathoners. Mr. Clive Davis of California started to run late in life. For the last six years he had improved his marathon yearly. His latest is the world record of 2:43:58 for 66-year-old men. Without the heart being the kind of organ that it is, these feats would not be possible.

Like every other muscle, the heart serves the body in its own fashion. From the viewpoint of running, the heart is the essential prime mover of the cardiovascular and respiratory systems. It moves the bloodstream that carries those fueling elements for energy. While the liver and the tissues of our leg muscles can store food material for exercise, there is virtually no reservoir within the body for the storage of oxygen. Whenever the demands of exercise require increased supplies of oxygen, the pumping heart responds by supplying additional oxygenated blood to the tissues.

Anatomy of the Heart

The heart is a double pump, composed of strong fibrous tissue, richly vascularized. Within the fleshy muscle, roughly the size of one's fist, are four partitioned chambers. The upper chambers, called atria, serve primarily to receive blood from the veins and force it through the valves leading into the lower chambers, or ventricles (see figure). The left side of the heart is responsible for pumping the oxygenated blood with its nutrients to all the tissues of the body. In making its rounds of the body, the blood completes what is called the systematic

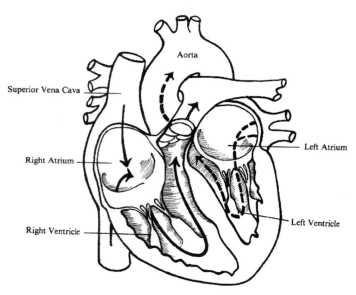

Chambers of the Heart

circuit. Equally important, and simultaneously proceeding, is the pumping by the right side of the heart. Its responsibility is to send the non-vitalized blood into the capillaries of the lungs for rejuvenation, after which it is then speeded back to the left atrium of the heart for systematic distribution. This part of the blood's movement is called pulmonary circuit.

These two complementary circuits work in an arc-like fashion to maintain the entire continuous flow of blood. Basically, the heart's complex pumping actions involve the two upper chambers filling with blood simultaneously. The chamber's relaxed phase (diastole) then contracts (systole), squeezing the blood medially "downstairs" into the relaxed lower chambers. These portions of the heart become overfilled, as it were, then undergo their own contraction. The blood now spurts from each side of these two ventricles to begin its circulatory route. As the blood leaves the lower chambers, a new vacuum is created above in the atria, allowing the cycle to commence again. The heart is again refilled with blood and the cardiac cycle proceeds with relaxation and contraction (see figure 5). This rhythmic pattern of the heart's circulatory efforts is expressed in the heartbeat or pulse rate. The call to running makes the heart pump blood faster (minute volume) and, with training, efficiently in larger amounts (stroke volume). This increased cardiac output enables the legs to fulfill the intention of the runner.

The heartbeats per minute can vary in healthy people. Even well-conditioned runners may have a higher resting rate that expected. Usually the heartbeat tends to decrease as the runner's condition improves, indicating that the heart is becoming stronger and can thus pump adequately with less effort. Not only does the heart improve its muscular state, but all its collateral associates, namely, the various types of blood vessels, undergo a vigorous transformation. Runners often find that the improvement of the cardiovascular system results in a lowering of their resting blood pressure.

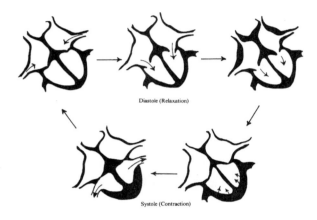

Diastole (Relaxation)

Systole (Contraction)

The Cardiac Cycle

The more the runner carries out a consistent program of weekly running, the more the heart has the opportunity to become stronger and improve its vital capacities. Systematic exercising of the heart will promote a moderate enlargement of its size over a period of time. An untrained adult heart measures in the area of 600 cubic centimeters. An Olympian distance runner's heart may be double that of his non-running neighbor's in size.

The heart of Armin Hary, the Olympic 100-meter winner, measures at 606 cubic centimeters, while Steve Prefontaine, Olympic finalist at 5000 meters, increased his heart size to 1205 cubic centimeters. The heart's healthy growth is reflected in a decreasing resting pulse rate and an increase output in the stroke volume. This latter development means that the heart can now squeeze a larger amount of blood with each contraction. More oxygen is now available to the running muscles with less expenditure by the heart.

The muscular composition of the heart is unusual; it does not give a graded performance. The arm or leg muscles may employ different degrees of tension. One can lift a weight and modify the tension of the biceps muscle during the lifting. The heart, on the other hand, gives all or nothing. Whether sitting at home or racing ten kilometers, the heart will always beat at its strongest contraction for its condition.

At rest or in casual walking, the volume of blood (about 5 liters) being pumped through the heart per minute may be five to eight times less than when the heart is called upon for running. Equally the heart rate may double, triple, or more under the intensity and duration of running. A consistent and moderate pressure upon the heart to increase its output gradually improves its capacity to disperse the oxygenated blood. A healthy heart is a remarkable adaptable organ in the face of moderate intensities of exercise. In their renowned studies in physiology, Drs. Moorhouse and Miller insist that "a healthy heart is never damaged by progressive endurance training." Granted that there are other factors influencing the heart's performance—the emotional attitude toward the run, the environmental temperature, and the physical condition of the runner—it is important to explore further the vital coordination between the heart and breathing that keeps the runner running.

Often, beginning runners have heard about a formula for gauging safe heart rate during their workouts. Two well-know physiologists, B.O. Ostrand and R. Rodahl, proposed a scale for the maximum heart rate during exercise in reference to one's age. Running books borrow this scale and advocate subtracting your age from the general human maximum of 220 beats for minute to obtain your apparent maximum. The objective is to run only so fast that the heart rate remains within 60-85 percent of this personal maximum. By staying within this range, one is supposedly assured of safe running for the heart and for its natural development.

The scale is not meant to be an absolute measurement, but an average estimate. Considerable variation exists among people, however, so that the rise in the heart rate during running can differ widely. For some people vigorous exercise may accelerate the heart rate within five minutes or less near maximum, while others may continue to note a slow rise in pulse rate and a leveling off for the duration of the workout. Two controlling factors enter the picture: the type of running and the degree of fitness of the runner. For the beginning runner to sprint, rush hard up hills, or allow his breathing rate to become erratic, increases the heart rate needlessly and tires the runner. Easy running with rhythmic breathing allows the cardiovascular system to make its healthy adjustments over a period of time. As the months go by, the more fit the runner becomes, the more the increase in cardiac efficiency becomes evident in a given workout. In a well-conditioned heart the stoke volume is greater, and thus less pumping is required to supply oxygen to the leg muscles. The heart works less, and with greater production with each contraction.

In respecting the healthy development of cardiac endurance, the runner needs to pace himself without excessive intensity. Taking one's pulse is one way to measure intensity, but there is a better check. Running in a steady state of consistent breathing accomplishes proper cardiac development and at the same time increases one's concentration upon rhythmic breathing. Running in a steady breath state avoids straining the internal organs while gradually improving the present bodily condition. By setting a running pace according to the breathing, one can constantly monitor the perceived exertion and the heart's need for oxygen. In this way, the present conditioning stage is developed and endurance progressively increases without over-exerting the runner.

In concentrating on rhythmic breathing, one acquires a certain interior "feel" for training without strain. One should modify the pace throughout the workout so that one's present breath limits are not exceeded. If any shortness of breath is noted, or if one hears the pounding of the heart while running, the pace should be slowed. With breath-paced running, neither the heart nor the lungs are unduly taxed beyond their current capacity. On the contrary, the endurance of the heart, lungs, and leg muscles improves progressively as well as synergistically, over the weeks, without uncomfortable stress or fatigue. By regulating the breathing one sustains a safe aerobic pressure upon the entire body.

During easy, rhythmic breathing, the heart receives sufficient oxygen to adjust its pumping rate to the pace of steady running. When oxygen is supplied to the heart in adequate amounts to avoid oxygen debt, the heart rate remains relatively less accelerated, because of the efficient way the runner breathes. Running in this manner illustrates the physiological principle that heart rate is directly related to oxygen uptake.

Breath, Heart Rate, Oxygen Supply, and Pace

During rest and running the heart rate is regulated by a complex interplay involving both nerves and chemical factors. Unlike the body's skeletal muscles, which depend upon the nervous system for their excitation, the human heart has a certain independence from the nervous system in its movement.

Yet the heart also contains two types of cardiac nerves which have an important influence by the vagus nerve (the tenth cranial nerve of the parasympathetic system) to slow the beating rate. The heart also displays sympathetic nerves which increase the beating rate. It is the antagonistic interactions between these nerves that stimulate the heart's activity.

The vagus impulses arise from the medulla portion of the brain, which can be immediately influenced by the breathing rate. As the heart performs through a session of steady running with rhythmic breathing, it tends not to accelerate as fast as it did at the beginning of the running program. The heart muscle is being toned up; it is improving its vagal tone. Since the breathing proceeds rhythmically and aerobically, the medulla does not send impulses for the sympathetic increase of the heartbeat to provide additional oxygen.

Vagal action upon the heart is associated with diaphragmatic breathing rather than upper chest breathing. The later activates the sympathetic nerves which excite the heart rate. Obviously, in running some amount of accelerator or sympathetic tone persists, but its influence on the beating rate is overshadowed by that of the vagal impulses, making for easy running and rhythmic breathing.

Diaphragmatic breathing correlates with the vagus impulses, which in turn maintain a lower heart rate. Since one is not attempting very strenuous running, there is no need to stimulate the sympathetic nerves any more than minimally. The runner continues in a steady, aerobic state. One's reserves are untouched.

Often runners starting out put a completely unnecessary strain upon themselves. They somehow think that punishing the body is the best way to become fit! By this approach, a runner can, in opposition to steady vagal action, arouse the sympathetic system to speed the heartbeat. For races, and for improving tolerance to the anaerobic condition, this type of accelerator influence can be carefully involved. Running for fitness, however, eschews this type of stressful running.

In following the steady breath program outlined in this book, emphasis remains upon the movement of the diaphragm and not the upper chest muscles. Forceful breathing with the chest calls into play unnecessary muscular efforts and corresponding increased beating of the heart. A false emergency exists. The excessive ventilation serves no beneficial purpose for gentle running, since the delivery of oxygen to the tissues is limited by the maximal output of blood by the heart as well as the vessels' capacity for receiving the flow of blood. Forcing the heart to work harder than necessary does not help the runner. When the heart of an unconditioned runner beats at a higher rate, for example at 165, it may not be operating efficiently, since the chambers are not filling and emptying fully. The heart is working harder to sustain a running pace that could have been achieved with less cardiac effort by rhythmic diaphragmatic nasal breathing.

An additional strain can likewise occur as high heartbeats indicate that the runner is approaching an anaerobic condition. The body requires a constant chemical balance known as the blood pH level. Running metabolism sustains this delicate balance when there is sufficient oxygen. As the runner tires, the lungs get rid of most of the excessive acids by blowing them off in the form of carbon dioxide. But this excretory route is limited and needs the kidneys to buffer the blood and maintain the chemical balance against acidic conditions forming in the blood. Unfortunately high thoracic breathing tends to reduce kidney function, and the body reduces its buffer defense against the formation of acidosis. A toxic condition emerges which the runner's muscles cannot tolerate for long; hence the runner becomes easily fatigued.

Breathing rapidly and producing a higher heart rate tires the runner faster through excessive oxygen consumption and eventually makes running a distasteful experience. Running in an easy stress-free manner, giving free play to the diaphragmatic breath rhythm as the guiding factor, avoids burdening the heart. This intercoordination between breath rhythm, ample oxygen supply, heart rate, and a relaxed pace enables one to avoid excessive exertion and to progress toward optimal fitness with ease.

The discharge of impulses from the vagal or cardio-inhibitory center in the medulla is also influenced by the portal of breathing. Breathing through the nose provides the inner brain—the limbic system—with an immediate supply of energy. As the air enters the nasal passages it immediately stimulates the inner brain. A constant supply of sufficient oxygen enables the runner to remain emotionally calm, while activating the production of the body's opiates or painkillers to modify the normal stress associate with endurance running.

Daily, sensible running tones and increases the functional endurance of the heart. A gentle pace eases the body into adjusting itself to the demands of the workout. There is less shock upon the nervous system, for one's nervous reserves are not depleted. Running in a steady breathing state allows the cardiovascular system to extend its present threshold, improving the performance of its arteries and capillaries and even developing new capillaries in the heart and leg muscles. The continual demand from the leg muscles for oxygen stimulates the heart's efficiency. When you run frequently, the heart gets stronger in its performance, pumping oxygenated blood at a better rate than an unconditioned heart.

As your running program continues, your resting heart rate will indicate its improved fitness by slowly reducing its beats per minute. Over a six-month period of consistent running, you may notice that your resting heart rate is possibly ten beats less than when you began the program. Fewer, but stronger, heartbeats are now available for supplying the oxygen to your body throughout the day.

To enjoy running, one needs to build up the heart's ability to transport oxygen, and thus become virtually tireless. Children romp through hours of play, not by running fast all the time, but by taking rest through walking. This principle is just as sound for adults. Exertion and pause guides intelligent running, Pushing yourself, accelerating the heartbeat, and becoming breathless, generates neither enjoyment not relaxed improvement, Interspersing your running with creative walks whenever you feel tired keeps you fresh by giving the heart and leg muscles a chance to restore themselves. Improvement is not meant to be a constant strain upon the body. The entire body responds better to prolonged running mixed with walking at a moderate pace, than by making the heart accelerate with harsh, breathless running.

Two Experiments in Rhythmic Breathing

Two men, ages 27 (subject A) and 47 (subject B) began a running program using diaphragmatic nasal breathing. The younger man ran approximately 30 minutes a day, averaging five to six days a week. He ran consistently at an even breath ratio, coordinating his breath cycle with his steps. He exhaled for six steps and then inhaled for six steps. Monitoring himself, he started the program with a resting pulse of 72 beats per minute. After four months of running, the resting pulse decreased to the low 60's (see chart 1). He checked his pulse at the mid-workout period each day. His pulse during mid-workout went from a high of 144 per minute to a gradual decrease to the low 120's at the end of the fourth month (see chart 2). He averaged a 12-minute per mile pace.

The second man, subject B, started out from a very sedentary lifestyle. His resting pulse was 75 beats per minute. Slow running and walking were mixed for 40-50 minutes a day on the basis of five to six days per week. At the end of a four-month period, his resting heart rate decreased to 60 beats per minute (see chart 1). The running heart rate at mid-workout fluctuated between 138-150, depending upon the length and intensity of the workout. At no time did he try to push himself. After the first two weeks of adjusting the breathing rhythm, all running was done at a 2:1 breath ration, exhaling twice as long as inhaling at a 6-step to 3-step proportion. At the end of six months, subject B could easily run five miles at a pace of 91/2 minutes per mile. Later, after ten months of running, he ran 9 miles in 71 minutes, keeping the breath ration at a steady 6:3 rate. He averaged 18-20 breaths per minute throughout the run and was not at all breathless at its completion. Running heartbeat was 144 at completion.

Both runners avoided anaerobic running. They ran as they felt inclined, but kept the consistency in terms of length of work out and rhythmic breathing. Both noticed over the months that their recovery rate and corresponding feelings improved. They recovered faster to their resting heart rate form their daily exertions. In subject A's case, the body weight stabilized during his winter running. Likewise, subject B lost a few pounds in weight and then stabilized. No major alterations in diet occurred during these months. Progress in endurance came without severe exertion.

Chart 3 indicates the gradual progress of subject B in reference to his ability to lower the time for a mile while extending his endurance each week. Using the sense of perceived exertion as governed by rhythmic breathing, he slowly improved from the first week of quarter-mile segments, at best, to running continuously for 7 to 8 miles by the 20th week. The speed increased easily, from 16 minutes per mile to 71/2 to 8 minutes per mile. Heart rate was very constant, between 144-50 at the completion of the daily workouts.

To expand your threshold of endurance without strain, run with a rhythmic breath. In this way you will be able to do longer workouts and feel less tired than expected. In under a year, one can easily work out for an uninterrupted hour of comfortable aerobic running.

Thanks to the heart's natural propensity as an endurance muscle, steady rhythmic breathing feeds it the necessary oxygen for continual improvement. Interestingly, a sprinter's heart seldom exceeds the size of that of a sedentary youth. Sprinters develop powerful leg muscles but rarely have endurance. It is not the speed but the steady duration that forges healthy organs. Master coach Arthur Lydiard says in reference to endurance, "The development of stamina is of the greatest importance, to have the body in a tireless state so that an oxygen debt is not quickly created and recovery power is rapid". With prolonged movement of comfortable intensity the heart can develop its potential for endurance.

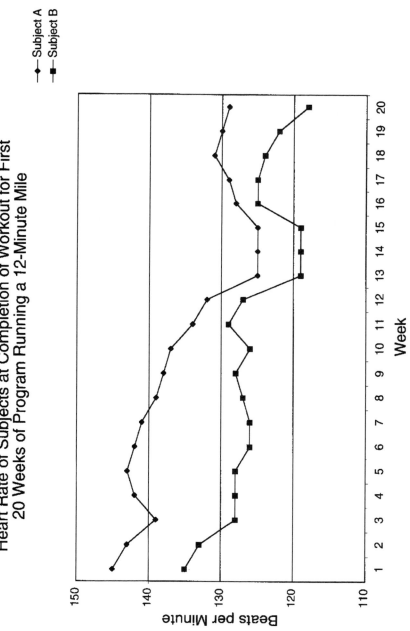

Heart Rate of Subjects at Completion of Workout for First
20 Weeks of Program Running a 12-Minute Mile

Subject A
Subject B

Beats per Minute

Week

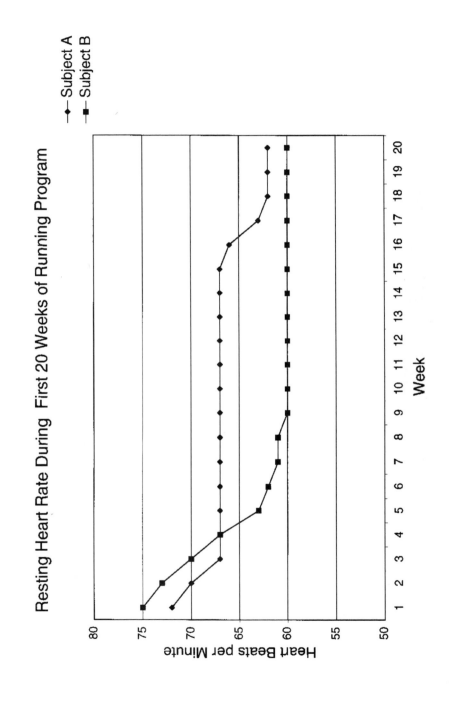

Resting Heart Rate During First 20 Weeks of Running Program

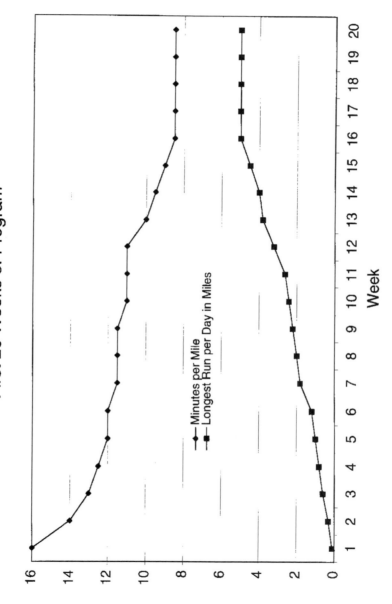

Speed and Mileage of Subject B During
First 20 Weeks of Program

Minutes per Mile
Longest Run per Day in Miles

Week

5
The Workout

Running is not complicated, but developing your workout requires an intelligent mix of various elements. A running program designed to improve health and attain fitness through endurance at any age requires that one understand and apply the dynamics of running with rhythmic breathing.

Either before you get out to run or during your beginning workout, settle the question, "Why am I running?" Running can and should be fun, but if you are intrigued with the possibilities of running as a performance for life long health, you must take your play more seriously. Being playful but serious is not being rigid in following your workout—the lightness is there but so is the intelligent understanding of what you are doing with yourself, and the willingness to make adjustments in your running on the spot as you sense it is necessary. Let this approach become your philosophy of running.

The attempt to sprint repeatedly in daily running is not the way to begin an intelligent program for a lifetime. To sprint, to run hard or breathe erratically, to the point of becoming tight, tired, and resentful are abusive in the long run, wasted motion, and poor thinking. 'No pain, no gain' is stupid and self-defeating. The human body is an extraordinary flexible entity which can endure a lot of punishing workouts and still improve its performance. But whether you desire to risk eventually injuring the body, or to embark on an intelligent and challenging pursuit of physical excellence comes down to the matter of attitude. Your sense of competition for an occasional road race won't be diminished by taking a balanced approach. Keep competitive feelings out of your daily running; it blights your enjoyment and becomes self-destructive to your motive. More runners have eventually quit running due to the painful consequences of driving themselves in practice than any other motivating factor.

In high school and college, my experiences with the coaches nearly terminated my running career. The high school coach was primarily the football mentor, with track being one of his other marginal duties, so he coached track by reading from a book, being careful not to admit his lack of background in running. His position was that if you could not duplicate the prescribed times per workout which were listed in his book, then you could not stay on the team. Unless you neared the state records, you would not be permitted to try out for the city championship. As a result, there were no running contests with other schools. No one was good enough.

At my university, the coach was himself a superb runner, an Olympian, but his coaching approach insisted that everyone follow the same pattern of workouts. Whether one started running in October or May, whether one was a sprinter or a long-distant runner, the approach was the same: racing daily with team members week after week. The coach was convinced that daily competition was the best way to get the team ready for the meets. By the end of the season, you were weary of running. Only one runner from the team continued to run after graduation.

Your training workout should be enjoyable. It's all in the approach. Keep competition out of it. Instead, play at your running.

Train yourself with light-heartedness, exploring creative interludes of walking, stretching, and running. Enjoy yourself in the experience and your workout will produce enduring fruits.

Runners are usually interested in increasing speed. It is paradoxical that sustained speed is attained by ignoring it and concentrating instead on endurance. If the runner faithfully follows his careful schedule of endurance-building, speed will take care of itself as a natural outcome. Peter Snell, a gold medals winner in the Olympics, says in *No Bugles, No Drums,* "I believe that virtually any form of speed running which is going to accustom the body to the demands of racing at pace over a particular distance is going to bring the athlete through to form once he has laid the foundation of stamina and condition." Foster endurance and the speed will show up later.

Breath Leads the Pace

Running with rhythmic breathing does not require use of the mouth. Full exhalation and inhalation can occur entirely through the nostrils. No doubt this approach appears strange or unorthodox. Many people do not use the nostrils for every breath nor employ the diaphragm as their normal custom of breathing. Since they are indifferent to their resting breathing rate, it probably comes as an awkward surprise to hear of breath regulation for optimal health during exercise.

To accustom yourself to rhythmic breathing while running and discover how easily the body accepts diaphragmatic nasal breathing, always keep in mind that breath leads the pace. This means that the running pace follows upon the steady rhythm of the breath, not the other way around. Don't breathe to keep up with the pace; pace yourself to coordinate with breath rhythm. Breathing leads leg movement.

When you begin your program, the pace should be quite slow with a lot of interspersed walking. In the section on daily schedules which follows, explicit details are given to accustom the beginner to this new approach through walking. Once you have become familiar and comfortable with breathing diaphragmatically through the nostrils, then your pace naturally picks up. Running slowly at first gives you a great advantage: it allows you time to adjust the breathing to a comfortable rhythm. At first, the rhythm should be even, with the exhalation and inhalation approximately the same length. Sustain this ratio 1:1 for some time. Don't hold your breath anywhere along the way; breathe continuously, without any pause. Later, when the even, nasal, diaphragmatic breathing rhythm becomes almost second nature to you, gradually readjust your breathing to a 2:1 ratio of exhalation to inhalation. That means that you now exhale for twice as long as you inhale. This can be the normal breathing rhythm throughout your entire workout.

Directing the breath to lead the pace insures the proper coordination between heart and lungs and legs. Rhythmic breathing keeps the pulse rate at an economical range that prevents overstressing the heart, blood vessels, and nervous system. By sustaining balanced breathing, especially at the eventual 2:1 ratio, optimal oxygen transport is supplied through the circulatory system. There is no reason to emphasize the upper chest or thoracic portion of your body; both will take care of themselves. As we have seen, emphasizing chest breathing demands additional energy, making the heart and nervous system work harder.

Discover for yourself that you cannot incur an oxygen debt with steady, rhythmic breathing. With it you guide your running by awareness of the feeling that emerges from the rhythmic breathing. As long as your breath can be sustained smoothly, you are developing endurance at an optimal rate.

At the beginning, you might notice a shortness of breath during the workout. Perhaps your legs seem to hold out longer at this period of your development than your lungs. Either way just take it easy. You are not in a rush. Gradually you will find that the lungs are becoming more efficient than the legs. Although the body is getting stronger, not every part acquires fitness at the same rate of development, so keep your philosophy of running in mind.

Run with ease. Run slowly. Allow the breath to maintain its regular pattern. Interject frequent periods of walking. Remember that the object of a good workout is not to reach such a stage that you have to drag yourself to the shower. When you feel good about the workout, when you have a sense of pleasant tiredness, when you have enjoyed the outdoors, when you look forward to the next workout, then you have had a successful time. Eventually, you will feel that you can extend yourself further, your legs and lungs will then be ready and will easily perform.

Running Without Tension

Running daily at a relaxed pace with easy breathing produces amazing physiological changes for the better. When the breath flows at a consistent ratio, the body easily adapts to the moderate stress of running. By not forcing the pace nor seeking the stimulus of competition, one eliminates emotional strain. Then towards the middle or near the end of an hour workout, the balanced breathing and casual attitude of the runner often produces a feeling of mild exhilaration. This welcomed feeling is more likely to recur as the runner achieves an improved state of fitness, usually after six to ten weeks. By always starting the workout with very slow and easy running, and by inserting frequent walks, the body has ample time, in its own way, to adjust itself to the moderate exertion of the day.

During the workout you may feel a breathing discomfort When tiredness occurs, recheck your breathing pattern and either slow down or move into a walk until you feel restored. With careful monitoring of the breath rhythm through daily workouts, the onset of muscular or breathing stress is more and more diminished, and gradually looses intensity. Diminishing fatigue signals the development of endurance.

Always finish a workout knowing full well that you could have run faster and farther. The way to insure this reaction is to depart for the shower before exhaustion. Or decide on a given period of time for your workout, and quit at that time, even if you feel you have hardly run. You will enjoy the experience of running more by underestimating your endurance than by pushing yourself to fulfill a predetermined schedule. Your schedule—how far, how fast—is only a guide, a very flexible guide.

Run by the way you breathe, knowing that there are days when it takes some time before you feel in the mood to run. You may have to "tease" and coax the body awhile. Jog slowly for short distances. Walk awhile. Jog some more, but easily, without strain. Be patient with the body. Don't punish yourself. There are no running police demanding, "Run or else!"

As the circulation increases through your body vessels and you become warmer, the mood of your body will change, accepting your intention. The accelerated heartbeat, the regulated breath flow, the loosening and movement of various muscles generate a tonal quality in the body that eases you into the running mood. Some days it is the body that resists and other days it is the mind. In either case, take it slow and ease into the workout. Just putting on your running shoes sometimes tilts the mood in your favor. Don't expect much; just get out there. Sometimes the day you feel least like running may turn out to be one of your most exhilarating experiences.

Flexibility

An index of health and strength is the suppleness of the body. Running performance will definitely be improved by increasing the flexibility of the leg muscles. Both the relief and the prevention of muscle soreness and joint strain can be achieved by supplementing your workout with stretching exercises and hatha yoga postures.

Rapid stretching, or allowing another person to pull or push you into a stretch increases the chances for injury. The use of jerky or bouncing movements provokes a very intense reflex contraction against the direction of the stretch. These rapid, forceful movements do not increase flexibility as much as they strain and bruise muscles and tendons. The objective of stretching is not to withstand pain and tension, but to progress toward suppleness. The most beneficial way to strengthen and increase muscular flexibility is to perform the postures slowly, with full attention, and breathing calmly.

By easing into and out of the stretch, muscles are brought to their maximum extension. The stretch is extended in its particular direction until tightness, not pain, is felt. At this juncture, one should hold the posture and relax into it, as it were, by breathing diaphragmatically for 20 seconds to a minute.

By breathing evenly and comfortably and by sustaining the extension of the stretch, the normal tension of the reflex contraction gradually subsides. In this relaxed condition, one can extend the stretch slightly farther until one feels tightness again. What is crucial for the development of flexibility is the relaxed, painless sustentation of the stretch. Never force the posture into a feeling of pain and increased tension. By doing the stretching exercise slowly, less tension occurs in the muscles, and over a period of weeks the relaxed posture safely allows for future extension.

The Three Phases of Running

Conditioning is a matter of improved adaptation. The following monthly schedule offers a guide to the typical beginner who is in poor condition. Improving condition means extending the body slightly past its present limits of comfortable endurance. When running is performed over a period of weeks—at least three times weekly—the accumulated impact has its most beneficial effect.

The first phase of running is basically getting the beginner used to integrating breathing with leg movement at an even ratio for 20

20 minutes. Depending on the person's physical condition and the degree of interest, the integration will proceed almost immediately, or at most after a few days. Just about everyone can breathe rhythmically if they put their mind to it.

The weeks of phase one, then, are the initial days of getting the body and the muscles used to exercise on a regular basis. Some temporary soreness can be expected before the tissues toughen to the new demands being made upon them. With the recommended stretching and massaging, any stiffness will diminish and the legs will become more supple.

Phase two is the transition to a breathing ratio in which the runner exhales for twice as long as s/he inhales. One should reach this juncture after about a month of workouts. For some people it may take longer (two months or more) to acclimatize the respiratory system to rhythmic breathing.

At this point the runner should not be concerned with how fast s/he is running. This will now become a temptation, since endurance is improving, but speed is useless as a gauge of progress. The acquisition of endurance comes with repeated exposure to frequent, easy running for many minutes. Rather than increase the pace to a state of heavy breathing, one should run longer as he feels stronger in this phase. Slower, longer runs, interspersed with lots of walking, are the way to fastest progress.

The third phase of running means the runner is capable of sustained easy, long runs. Generally, one will come to this level after nine to fifteen months of continuous practice. One indication that one is ready for this transition to longer runs is the ease of doing 400-meter runs with full recovery of 15-20 repetitions without feeling fatigued. Once the runner is conditioned to the level of fitness where s/he can easily handle 3 1/2 miles of 400-meter segments with a sense of full recovery, then long runs are around the corner.

With the above thoughts in mind, examine the following schedule for guidance. No schedule can anticipate every runner's physical background, but once you take your first steps, your body will inform you better than any external measure when to go on. Use the schedule according to your common sense of how you feel, which will grow keener as you practice. Take an easy, but steady, commitment to your practice. The summary below will indicate general guidelines at a glance.

WEEK	WORKOUT	COOLDOWN	TIME
1	Walk for 20 min. Even, diaphragmatic breathing. Intersperse with brisk walking.		20 min.
2	Walk 20-50 meters; jog 20-50 meters. Even, diaphragmatic breathing.	Introduce stretches	20 min.
3	Walk 50 meters; run 50-100 meters. Brisk walking. Even, diaphragmatic breathing.	Stretches Postures	30 min.
4	Walk 50-150 meters; run 50-150 meters.	Stretches Postures	30 min.
5-8	Walk 50-300 meters; run 50-300 meters. Introduce 2:1 breathing.	Stretches Postures	40 min.
9-12	Mix walking and running from 50-400 meters. Introduce long runs of 3-5 min. Continue 2:1 breathing. Vary the pace.	Stretches Postures	45 min.
Beyond 12 wks.	Increase long runs to 10-15 min. Later intersperse long runs to 20-60 min. or more. Recovery walks. Continue 2:1 breathing. Vary pace / distance according to condition.	Stretches Postures	45 min.+

Variations are welcome. Grasp the principles guiding the schedule and adjust them to your age, condition, and circumstances.

SCHEDULES

Week One

Running begins with walking. To ease into running promotes an enjoyable experience. It is necessary to adopt a progressive approach. Go out for a walk. You don't have to dress up in any special garb, but wear a good pair of comfortable walking shoes. That's the only item you really need. Start out with a 20-minute walk.

Breathe diaphragmatically as you walk, keeping the lips sealed. After 5 minutes, streamline your breathing. Exhale and inhale evenly. Measure your breath rate in terms of the steps that your feet are taking. For example, exhale for 3 or 4 steps and then inhale for 3 or 4 steps immediately after. Adjust. You are attempting to synchronize your breathing with your gait. Start slowly; coordinate the breathe with the steps. What is important here, in the beginnng, is that the coordination between the breath and walking should feel rhythmic. Don't lift or puff up your chest. Don't force your breath in order to match your steps, and don't hurry your steps to keep up with your breathing. Experiment; find your rhythm. Allow your breathing cycle to be natural and free, but with enough regulation to maintain an easy, even, coordination between walking and breathing.

Try this for 50-100 meters or so. Note how it feels. If it seems awkward or too complicated, start all over again. Do it slowly this time. It may take some days before a beginner will ease into a breathing rhythm that expresses the coordination of breath and leg movement. Swing your arms naturally, hold your upper torso erect, and simply walk. Emphasize the rhythm. Enjoy the walk. Twenty to thirty minutes a day is sufficient to accustom the respiratory system to its new habit of rhythmic breathing. You may feel upon the termination of your walk that you want to go on longer. But that feeling should be preserved, and the best way to preserve it is to taper off the workout now. In other words, we want you to come back again tomorrow.

Try to find a level ground to walk on. Don't just walk up hills; they are too difficult at this juncture. The additional strain of lifting your legs will interfere with the smooth breathing pattern you want to establish. Obviously the local terrain cannot always be as level as we wish for our purposes, but as a general rule, roads are better than grass. Grass is acceptable, but you may have to slow down a bit on it since it is usually not very level, and often scattered with holes and depressions. You are better off on the sidewalk, on a dirt road, or even in an empty parking lot. The firmer the surface, the easier it is to maintain your gait.

Take advantage of your non-running hours by incorporating diaphragmatic breathing throughout the day; let it become your norm of breathing. Your daily practice will slowly build a new habit; your breathing will gradually become deeper and smoother, producing a feeling of exhilaration when you complete your workout.

Repeat this first week, again and again if necessary, until you feel at ease with diaphragmatic nasal breathing. Only then should you attempt the second week of training.

Week Two

As in the first week, maintain a 20-minute workout during this week. But now you will be more creative. Instead of only walking, you will slowly introduce easy, comfortable jogging. The addition of running should not disturb what you have already achieved by your walking. You are merely beginning to lift the body into a running motion while maintaining the rhythmic breathing.

Be careful; you may want to run faster than your respiratory system is prepared to support. Since breathing is the focus of this training method, your speed is irrelevant; your concern is with maintaining a balanced breathing pattern. Experiment with adjusting your pace to your even breathing. Practically speaking, this may involve running slower than you have been walking. In fact, you may find the successful transition from walking to running becomes easier by jogging in an almost slow motion movement. In so doing, you will find it easier to maintain the rhythm of your breath in coordination with your jogging steps.

Here each person can decide, on the basis of smoothness of his or her own coordination, how to set the ratio. Jog for 20, 30, or 40 meters and then go back to a walk. Walk for another 50 meters or so and then jog again. Repeat these segments of walking and jogging for the remainder of your 20-minute workout. Play at it. If at any time you feel that you are forcing your breath, then return to walking. A few minutes later, when you feel at ease with yourself again, jog for another 10-50 meters.

In the middle of your workout, if the mood strikes you, stop to do some stretching exercises for about 5 minutes. Conditioning has nothing to do with harshness; it's the continuous movement at various intervals and variable pacing that eventually pays off.

By following this kind of progression, you allow the entire organism, the running muscles and physiology, to adjust to a mild exertion which increases your overall vitality. Since you won't be attempting to make the Olympic team in the first month or two, take the long-range viewpoint.

Remember to set up your goal of fitness or improvement or just enjoying bodily exercise for some months to come. In this way you avoid injury, undue stress, and the sickening feeling that often lingers in people when they try to press themselves beyond the limits of their current condition.

After a few days, make your running playful. By that I mean, allow your walking to be a little longer or brisker for a while, jog longer or shorter, but don't exceed 100 meters at a time. Make your segments variable. Feel as though you are performing an experiment in conditioning that will reveal more about yourself, while at the same time making the new discovery an energetic event.

Week Three

You may wish to work out longer now, but the purpose of the third week is not to test yourself nor bring your body to the brink of tension. The object is to become pleasantly tired. Therefore, when you return home, you should have come away from the workout feeling as though you could do more. This attitude, having been generated by your intelligent, easy approach, will motivate your subsequent workouts.

Again, begin by walking. After some minutes play with the walking speed. Do not race yourself; just increase the pace of your steps so that it would be difficult to do any casual window shopping. Can the breath remain rhythmical as you walk faster? Try brisk walking in small doses and see. Should you have a companion who is accompanying you, your pace should still enable you to hold a conversation without becoming out of breath.

Your breathing in the third week should become more comfortable than before. You may even find yourself readjusting the number of steps so that the coordination is lengthening out. For example, say that in the first week you were walking 2 steps to inhalation and 2 to exhalation. Now you might find yourself walking 3 to 4 or 5 steps of inhalation and exhalation.

Begin to introduce slow, easy jogging, up to 50-100 meters at a time. Gauge how you feel. Return to your walking until you feel you are recovered and then jog again, breathing evenly, easily, and smoothly, for a repeated 50 meters or so. The breathing rhythm should be undisturbed when you make the transition from walking to jogging and back again. Try to keep the breath as synchronized as possible with your steps. Always restrict the length of your jogging whenever you feel undue stress.

Week Four

Whether you are running every other day or daily, restrict your workout this week to 30 minutes. Urge yourself, without straining, to sustain your runs 50-100 meters at a time. When these lengths become easy for you, then go slower than usual and extend your runs to 150-200 meters. Vary the pace in this manner, interjecting recovery walks. You can be quite creative in your approach. You could run two sets of 50-meters each, then one 100-meter segment. Next, try one 50-meter segment, then a slow 150 meters, and then another 50 meters. Play with your distance. Continue like this for your entire workout. Always walk between the sets until you feel rested. Let your breathing rate indicate how fast you can manage the runs. Don't push yourself to run 150 meters at the same pace as you run 50 or 100 meters. By slowing down for the longer runs, you will be learning something about gauging pace. As the weeks roll by, your body becomes more adjustable to the current pace and you will notice an instinctive quickening in your running. Thus, on the days when you feel very energetic, try to slow down the pace but run for a longer segment.

It is very important that your daily workout include stretches at its completion. Consider doubling the stretching time at the end of the workout. If you have been stretching for 3-4 minutes in your workout, then do 6-8 minutes at the end. Muscles shorten with prolonged use. By stretching the muscle fibers slowly, you aid recovery, facilitate the circulation to rid the muscles of their waste products and thus minimize the soreness felt the next day. A little stiffnes will be felt from time to time, even among the most conditioned runners, but stretching exercises will minimize them.

Second Month

Now you should transition to a different breath ratio. The transition consists in gradually extending your exhalation longer than your inhalation.

The last 4-6 weeks have been a pre-conditioning for a modification in your breath cycle. By now see if you can handle jogging for nearly 200 meters—about a long city block—with comfortable breathing. The transition to the new ratio of breathing should be attempted only after you have been running at least one month at an even breath ratio (exhalation = inhalation). It should feel second nature to you.

Your new concern is to lengthen the exhalation, making it longer than the inhalation. First, implement the longer exhalation while walking. This is crucial. Use walking as the introduction to the transition. Walk at a comfortable pace that allows your breathing rate to maintain an exhalation longer than your inhalation. Measure the lengthening of your steps. If you walk comfortably, say at a 3:3 or 5:5 ratio, then extend the exhalation 1 or 2 steps more and your nervous system will accommodate the change. Speed up your walking for a few hundred meters; then walk briskly for a few miles accommodating the transition. Try this in all your walking for a week or two (or more) until you are comfortable with extending your exhalation walking slowly or briskly. Then experiment with small doses of running using the broader ratio.

If you are running, say, at a 2:2 or 3:3 ratio, try to lengthen exhalation to another step and keep the inhalation at the same comfortable 2 or 3 steps. Again, you may have to run slower than before when introducing the longer exhalation. You should know by now from experience that it is easier to adjust breathing when you run slower for awhile.

How far should you lengthen the exhalation? The eventual goal is 2:1. It will take a while to get there comfortably. For some people lengthening the exhalation so that it is twice as long as the inhalation may take weeks. Broadening the range from an even ratio to a 2:1 ratio is there for experimenting over time. Most important is that the diaphragmatic nasal breathing be maintained regardless of the ratio.

Continue to sustain your running pace for the next 4 weeks until you can sustain running in a steady, rhythmic breath for 200-300 meters. Walk and repeat it. Follow the workout with stretches.

Third Month

By now your entire body is becoming habituated to regular periods of running. Slowly extend your workout time as your other commitments permit. Get in at least 45 minutes. Your improvement in further conditioning is just a matter of practice.

It won't be long before you can easily manage to run for 400 meters without stopping. Once you can easily run this distance, then insert a few runs of 5-10 minutes' duration for two days a week. Start slower than usual and run without any sense of strenuous exertion. If you feel overly tired as a result, then do only one long run twice a week. Wait another three weeks before adding more longer runs.

Always listen to your body as you run. Don't eliminate recovery walks or stretches from your workout. Don't try to run an uninterrupted mile yet. Continue staggering your workouts from 50-800 meters. Do these runs at varying paces that allow you to maintain your running with rhythmic breathing. Keep your workout minutes playful.

Beyond the Third Month

All levels of enjoyable performance are awaiting your fidelity to practice. The past months have prepared you for expanding your runs. Increasing the duration of your run will not be a harsh shock to your body provided you ease into it. The following approach illustrates the proper adjustment.

After a day of rest, warm up with jogging, walking. Then, at a very slow pace, sustain your run for 5 to 15 minutes. Breathe rhythmically, and no matter how easy it feels when you start (and it will definitely seem slow), keep the pace almost ridiculously slow throughout the period. Should the breathing become congested, or should soreness develop in the legs, then slow the pace even more or reduce your movement to walking. Again, how fast you run is not of importance at this stage. When you achieve these longer runs, you will have proved to yourself the meaning of endurance through running within your breath.

Your workouts should continue to reflect changes in their composition as your fitness improves. Now long and short runs can be mixed according to your taste. The sound base of endurance running can lead you to runs of even longer duration, eventually from 20-30 minutes or even longer.

The months will bring you along to a faster pace as your condition strengthens. Your speed will become a function of your endurance. Occasionally, after well warmed up, play with the pace briskly for 50 to 400 meters, extending your breathing rhythm to its edge. Then recover with slow jogging and walking. Remember that being pleasantly tired is not to be exhausted. You are now familiar with the principles for improvement. Through your self-application of them you know your capacity at any moment. Your capacity will improve steadily as you run sensibly.

Beyond the First Year

For those who wish to run very long distances, train more than one hour daily. After a year's running, the body has stabilized its metabolism to include your workout and more. How long or how far you desire to run is a matter of extening yourself in daily practice. If you wish to enter races, the principles of running within the breath remain the same. Preparation for races will involve getting the body accustomed to the designated distance through the discreet use of speed trials; that is, timing yourself for varying distances. Anyone who considers eventually running a marathon can certainly train along the lines described in this book, but I would suggest giving yourself about two years to prepare the body and gradually accumulate the conditioning required for that long haul.

Pace Chart

If you are wondering how fast your training may be on any given day, you can easily discover your pace by consulting the Pace Chart. When you know the approximate distance and your time interval, then you can gauge your time for distances. The chart divides the mile into various segments of distance and its equivalence in time intervals. If you are running 200 meters in approximately 1 minute 30 second, then a full mile at that pace would be run in 12 minutes.

PACE CHART

You run a mile in	100 meters	200 meters	400 meters	800 meters	1200 meters
15 minutes	:56	1:52	3:35	7:30	11:15
14 minutes	:52	1:45	3:30	7:00	10:30
13 minutes	:48	1:37	3;15	6:30	9:45
12 minutes	:45	1:30	3:00	6:00	9:00
11 minutes	:41	1:22	2:45	5:30	8:15
10 minutes	:37	1:15	2:30	5:00	7:30
9 minutes	:34	1:08	2:15	4:30	6:45
8 minutes	:30	1:00	2:00	4:00	6:00
7 minutes	:26	:53	1:45	3:30	5:15
6 minutes	:22	:45	1:30	3:00	4:30
5 minutes	:19	:37	1:15	2:30	3:45

Warming Up Sequence

Warming up is preventative medicine. It prepares the runner for more vigorous exercise without the risk of injury. The following sequence should be done daily before the workout.

Run gently for 5-10 minutes. Allow your body temperature to rise. Don't run hard; jog slowly and walk briskly in order to increase your circulation. For innovation, include some slow, backward sections of running, mixing it with running sideways. Swing the arms up and around at the sides, across in front and back. Jog forward for 10 meters, then turn around and jog even slower backwards for another 10 meters.

When you jog backwards, the ball of the rear foot strikes the ground first and then the rest of the foot lowers itself to the ground as the other foot swings backwards. This procedure should be carried out in almost slow motion so that the full stretch of the Achilles tendon is achieved.

Running sideways consists of simply crossing one leg over the other for a few meters then turning the body so that the other leg takes the lead in crossing over. The backwards and lateral movements strengthen and stretch the muscles and tendons leading into the knee and ankle joints, including the iliotibial band on the side of the knee joints. The knee area needs to be strengthened in order to stabilize and support the movement of the joint.

With the preliminary jogging and upper body calisthenics, the legs and lower back will respond much quicker to stretching and enable you to dissipate stiffness. By taking the time to warm up slowly you will find that the normal ingredients of your workout come quite easily without a lot of resistance by the mind or a feeling of physical resistance by the body. Make sure that you take the normal time of 5 to 10 minutes for a warmup so no injuries occur—in spite of your desire to "get going."

The Cooldown

Just as performance is improved if the muscles have been warmed up before prolonged activity, so stiffness and soreness are lessened if the muscles, tendons, and ligaments are cooled down at the end of the workout. Muscles swell and shorten with prolonged use. Lactic acid, fluid, and other waste products accumulate in the region of use. The more unconditioned the body, the quicker these products accumulate. The accumulation of these metabolic products impairs the utilization of energy by restricting the flow of oxygenated blood to the affected areas. The muscles themselves are unable to relax completely and stiffness results.

To aid the body in recovering muscle relaxation and tissue maintenance, it is important to spend some minutes in stretching and massaging sore areas. Gentle yoga postures improve the circulation of blood to the afflicted areas, enabling the by-products of running to be diffused into and carried off by the blood. Some soreness may be felt afterwards, but it usually recedes after three or four hours. Whatever stretches or postures chosen, experience shows that performing them with attentive slowness best enables recovery.

The next section describes the postures that can be used in the cool-down. These have been selected for walkers and runners particularly, although not everyone will be able to utilize all of them.

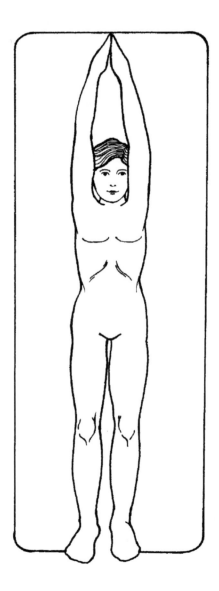

Overhead Stretch

Stand erect with your arms at your sides.

With an inhalation, raise the arms up over the head. Keep palms together and ears between the upper arms.

Without lifting the heels off the floor, stretch up from the legs, pelvis, and chest, reaching as high as you can.

With an exhalation, lower the arms and relax the body.

Arm Swings

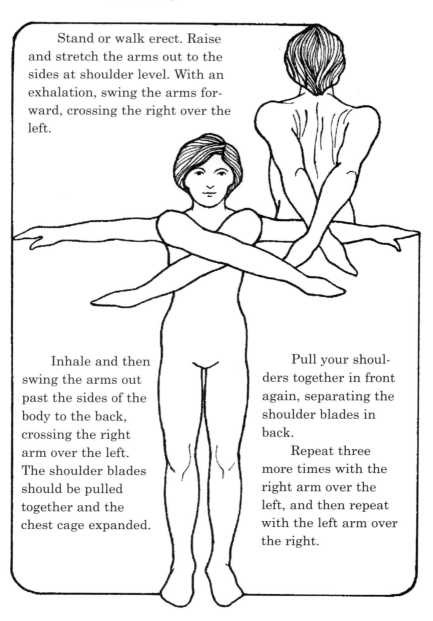

Stand or walk erect. Raise and stretch the arms out to the sides at shoulder level. With an exhalation, swing the arms forward, crossing the right over the left.

Inhale and then swing the arms out past the sides of the body to the back, crossing the right arm over the left. The shoulder blades should be pulled together and the chest cage expanded.

Pull your shoulders together in front again, separating the shoulder blades in back.

Repeat three more times with the right arm over the left, and then repeat with the left arm over the right.

Neck Rolls

Stand or sit erect. Exhale and slowly lower the head to the chest. Inhale and slowly roll the head up across the right shoulder and down across the back to the spine. Exhale and return to front.

Inhale and roll the head across the left shoulder and down across the back to the spine. Exhale and return to front. Repeat.

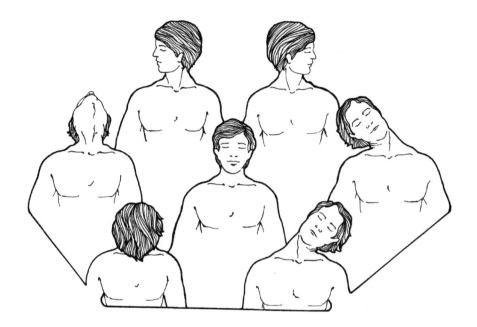

Neck Stretches

Stand or sit erect. While exhaling, slowly drop head to chest. Do not move the shoulders. Inhaling, slowly raise the head and drop it backwards, pointing the chin towards the ceiling. Inhale and return to center.

Exhale slowly and turn the head as far as possible to the right. Try to bring the chin over the shoulder, but do not move the shoulders. Inhale slowly and return to center.

Exhale and turn the head as far as possible to the left shoulder. Inhale and return to center.

Exhale and slowly lower the head to the right, trying to bring the ear to the right shoulder. Inhale and return to center.

Exhale while lowering the head to the left, and try to bring the left ear to the left shoulder. Inhale and return to center.

Stand erect with feet together. With an inhalation, bring hands and arms overhead, keeping arms close to the ears.

Exhale and bend forward from the hips keeping the back straight. Hold the toes with the fingers, or reach toward the toes.

Be sure to keep the spine straight, head between the arms. As much as possible, bring the head to the knees, but do not bend the legs.

Hold for three breaths.

With the next inhalation, raise the head, arms, and chest back to the erect form.

Standing Forward Bend

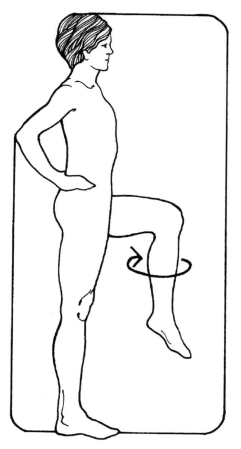

Stand erect with hands on the hips. Raise the right leg until the thigh is parallel to the floor.

Relax the leg, letting all the muscles below the knee hang loosely.

Swing the leg below the knee in a clockwise direction, keeping the thigh immobile.

Switch direction and swing the leg below the knee in a counter-clockwise direction.

Lower the leg to the floor and repeat the swirls with the left leg.

Knee Swirls

Stand erect with the hands on the hips.

Shift body weight to the left leg and raise the right leg slightly off the floor. Point the toes forward and then with a quick movement swing the right leg back to kick the buttocks.

Relax the leg and bring it down close to the floor. Then repeat the kick ten times.

Lower the right foot, shift the body weight to the right leg and kick ten times with the left leg.

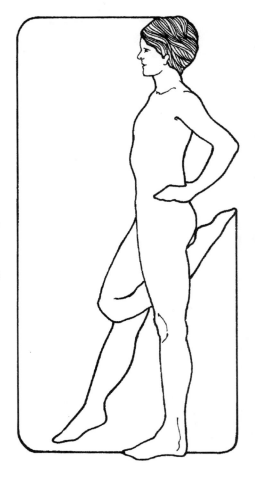

Leg Kicks

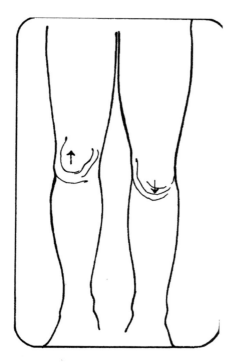

Dancing Knees

Stand erect, hands on hips, feet about ten inches apart. Then, by tensing the muscles above and surrounding the right kneecap, raise the kneecap. Relax muscles and let the kneecap return to its normal position. Repeat with the left kneecap.

Begin slowly and increase the speed of the motion. Continue to "dance" the knees for about one minute.

Ankle Rolls

Stand erect with hands on the hips. Shift body weight to the left leg. Keeping the right leg straight, raise it a few inches off the floor. Bending at the ankle, move the foot to point the toes up. Then slowly rotate the foot at the ankle in a clockwise direction and then in a counter-clockwise direction.

Lower the foot to the floor and relax. Shift body weight to the right leg. Repeat the entire exercise with the left foot.

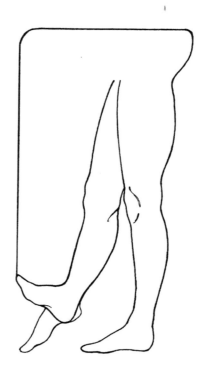

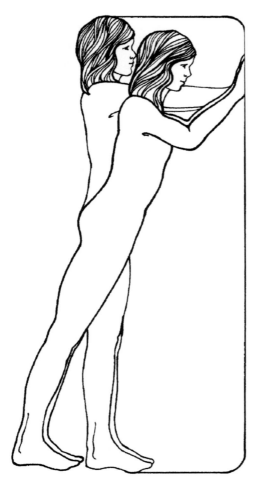

Wall Push Ups

Stand erect, facing a wall, about one foot away. Place your hands on the wall at shoulder level. Slowly walk backwards until your body is at a 45 degree angle. Keep your legs straight. Bend your arms at the elbow and lean into the wall, stretching the calf muscles. Breathe evenly for three breaths.

Extend your arms and repeat the exercise.

Next, bend your arms, leaning into the wall, but this time bend your knees forward, stretching the lower Achilles tendon. Hold for three breaths.

Return to the first position and repeat again.

King Dancer

Stand erect, arms at sides, and legs together. With an exhalation, bend the left leg and grasp the instep with the left hand. Pull the foot close to the buttocks. Inhale and lift the right arm straight up. With an exhalation, tilt the torso, head, and right arm forward as a unit. With the next inhalation, pull the shoulder blades together while holding the posture for three breaths.

With the next exhalation, slowly lower right arm, release left ankle, stand erect, and repeat on the other side.

Revolving Triangle

Stand erect, arms at sides, legs three feet apart.

Inhale and raise the arms to shoulder level, palms down while twisting the torso to the right.

With an exhalation, bend forward, placing the left hand along side the right foot and extend the right arm straight up. Look up at the right hand. Be sure not to bend the knees.

Breathe evenly for three breaths. With an inhalation, slowly rise to the standing position, arms at shoulder level.

With the next exhalation, repeat the bend on the left side, bringing the right hand alongside the left foot. Look up at the left hand and breathe for three breaths.

Return to the erect position.

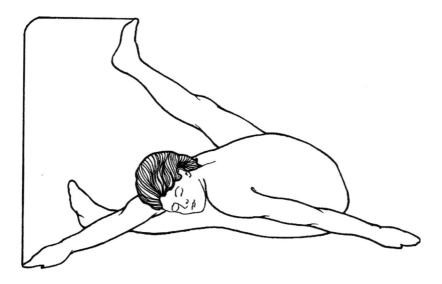

Churning

Sit erect with legs in front of the body as far apart as possible. With an exhalation, swing forward, touching the right hand to the left foot, while the left arm swings behind the back. During the swing, the body should lower to the knee while you look at the arm behind the back.

With an inhalation, return to an upright sitting position facing forward.

With the next exhalation, swing forward, touching the left hand to the right foot, right arm behind the back, while you look at the arm behind the back.

Continue this exercise several times, keeping up a quick, rhythmic, swinging movement.

Upraised Leg

Sit erect with legs extended, backs of knees flat on the floor. Place both hands on the right thigh. Slide the hands toward the right foot, simultaneously raising the leg toward the face.

Bring the leg as close to the face as possible, keeping the back straight. Do not bend the knees. Breathe evenly for three breaths. Lower the leg and relax.

Repeat this exercise with the left leg.

Leg Lifts

Lie on your back with your legs together, hands at side, and your palms on the floor. With an inhalation, raise the right leg as high as possible. Do not bend the knees. Hold for three breaths. With an exhalation, slowly lower the leg.

Next, as you inhale, raise the left leg as high as possible and hold for three breaths. Exhale and slowly lower the leg.

On an inhalation, raise both legs, keeping the knees unbent, and hold for three breaths. Exhale and slowly lower both legs.

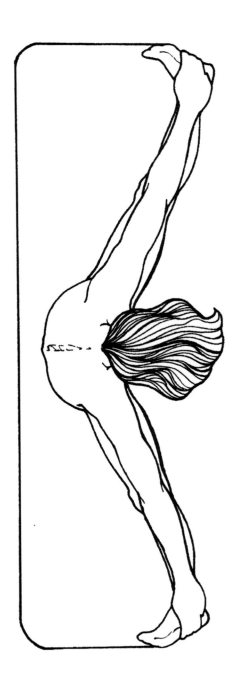

Spread Legs

Sit erect with the legs spread as far as possible, hands resting on the knees. With an inhalation, raise the arms out to the sides at shoulder level. With and exhalation, bend forward from the hips, trying to rest the chin on the floor. Grasp the instep of each foot. Breathe evenly for two to three breaths. With an inhalation, slowly return to a sitting position. Be sure to keep the spine straight during this posture.

Twisting Posture

Lie on your back, legs together, arms stretched out, palms down at shoulder level. With an inhalation, bend the knees and bring the legs up to the chest. With an exhalation, slowly lower the bent legs to the floor at the right elbow, while turning the head as far as possible to the left. Shoulders should remain on the floor. Breathe evenly for three breaths. With an inhalation, return the knees and head to the center. With the next exhalation, lower the bent legs to the floor at the left elbow, while turning the head as far as possible to the right. Repeat the exercise three times.

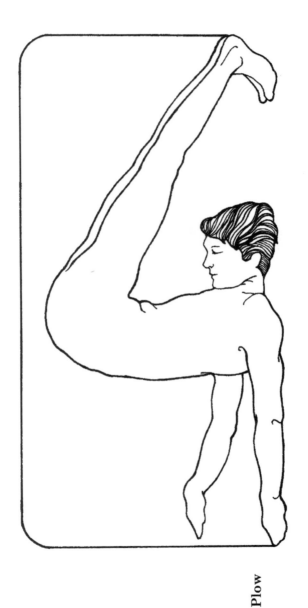

Plow

Lie on your back, arms at the sides and legs together. With an inhalation, slowly raise the legs perpendicular to the floor without bending the knees. Press the palms against the floor. Bring the legs back, raising the hips off the floor and finally the back. Keeping the legs together, slowly lower them to the floor behind the head. The arms remain on the floor. Breathe evenly for three breaths while holding the posture. With an exhalation, slowly lower the back, hips, and legs to the floor. Relax. Increase the time in this posture until you can hold it comfortably for one minute.

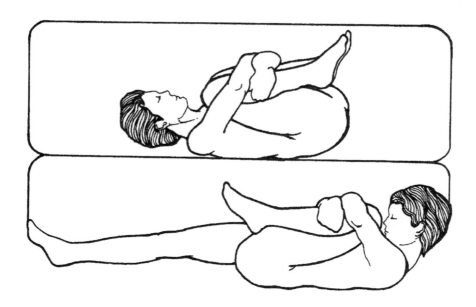

Knees to Chest

Lie on your back, legs extended. Bend the legs and bring them to the chest. Wrap your arms around the legs, pulling them as close as possible to the chest.

If there is any pain in the lower back, rock your body gently from side to side.

Next, extend the right leg to the floor, hold the left leg to the chest, and bring the forehead to the knee. Breathe evenly for three breaths.

Return to the prone position and then repeat practice with the other leg.

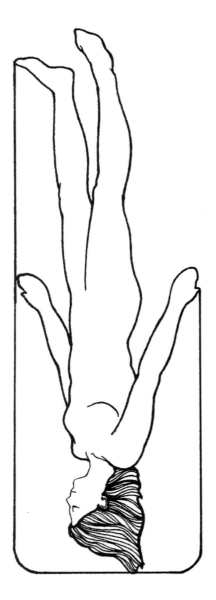

Corpse Pose

Lie on your back, legs about a foot apart, arms about eight inches from the body, palms up. The head, neck, and trunk should be in a straight line.

Close your eyes and relax the body completely. Breathe evenly and deeply for three to five minutes.

This posture should always complete any exercise series.

6

Injuries and Their Prevention

Injuries are a nuisance. But they can also serve a valuable purpose since they can tip off the runner as to his or her current condition. There is always a tendency lurking within that wants the runner to push farther and faster. It seems hard to resist the urge to pick up the pace or sprint the last portion of the workout. Runners often admit that they fantasize that they are in a race, and complete with a partner who has been running alongside them during a workout. Thus they set the stage for acquiring an injury.

While painless running is the goal, it is not exceptional to feel aches and stiffness occasionally. At first, unused muscles complain when one walks or runs beyond the accustomed range of endurance. Suddenly additional exertion is placed upon them and they quite naturally complain. It is like the first spring softball game, or the first autumn touch football contest. The exhilaration of getting out in the fresh air and running and playing with friends makes one feel as if the game could go on and on. But in the next day or two the unconditioned body returns the favor with pain.

No one likes to admit lack of fitness. Early expectations in any sport often overcome our common sense. It is not because one's body is too old that injuries occur, but simply that it becomes "rusty" through lack of use. Thus, we must forego fast running for awhile. Attempting to sprint when you are out of condition strains the entire body. Consequently, one is more likely to injure oneself seriously than at any other phase of the running program. There are some energetic moments that emerge spontaneously during the workout. This is fine, but the general rule is that gentle running and walking is the best insurance against straining the legs.

Exercise does not necessarily bring all parts of the body along at exactly the same rate of development. In beginning runners, the heart and lungs may improve before the legs. Many runners note that conditioning the heart and lungs seems to come earlier than getting the leg muscles in shape for distance running. The cardiovascular-respiratory system's positive response to daily running leads one to think that he can run a lot faster. But again it must be pointed out that the tendons, ligaments, and other connective tissues have to be exercised into condition more gradually.

The result of over doing it is generally felt in the joints and tendons, especially the knees, ankles, shins, and Achilles tendons. Very few people do not at one time or another feel some discomfort in these regions during their running career. This is not an occasion for alarm. With a little knowledge and a common sense running schedule, injuries can be avoided.

The best way to approach the possibility of minor discomfort is to take consistent preventative measures. One should always warm up carefully, that is, slowly, making sure that there is sufficient time to allow the entire body to prime itself into a state of running readiness. The capillaries need time to dilate; for most people this is about 10 to

15 minutes. Thus, stretches and exercises should not be done until the body is "warmed up."

Preventing Injuries

When you begin to run, you sometimes notices discomfort or pain. Legs become sore. Calf muscles tighten. Ankles and knee joints feel tender. The lower back hurts. In spite of the most gentle and cautious attention to slow, easy running, the legs stiffen after the run. That is because the muscles are being used in ways that put a new burden upon them and it takes timee for them to adjust to the added work.

The legs, like the rest of the body, are going through a reconditioning period. The increased movement, the further stretching of muscles and tendons, and the prolonged effort of the legs to accomplish the running objectives all draw upon the present state of one's condition while simultaneously improving it. In fact, as a general rule, if one feels mild discomfort one should not stop running. The workout should be continued, but at a slower, more restrained pace. Gentle, controlled running usually facilitates the healing and the strengthening of the mildly troubled region. Activating the muscles diminishes soreness faster than rest alone. In addition, the runner should supplement workouts with stretching exercises and massage.

The muscles ache because they need to gain more flexibility. Strength and flexibility go together. When muscles are supple they can apply their force more immediately and relax for efficient running. Since much of the tightness hampering the range of motion in the legs originates in the lower back, improving the flexibility of the back is imperative. Greater flexibility in the back and leg muscles can increase the length of a runner's stride as well as prevent injuries. A half-inch of improvement in flexibility saves about 65 yards per mile.

When a muscle is not used for a while it tends to shorten. That is, it decreases its flexibility and weakens its strength and capacity for work. To use it vigorously and intensely over a prolonged period also shortens it temporarily and produces a natural soreness that can last for a few days. The attempt to use the sore, stiffened muscles with the same degree of intense activity invites serious injury. To force a stiff muscle to do intense work, thinking one can push through the pain, is disastrous.

A question occurs here: How can one get past the soreness stage without further straining the muscles? The answer is a double sequence of common sense: the warm up and the cooldown. In their present condition the leg muscles have neither the strength nor the flexibility to sustain the workout that one will be doing three months hence. To prepare for these future workouts, and to provide continual conditioning, the muscles need stretching exercises, postures and massage that make up for the periods before and immediately after the workout.

The stretching in the warm up and cooldown session lengthens all the muscle fibers and improves flexibility, thus minimizing injury. Usually when one begins stretching, it becomes quite apparent that the extension isn't as far as one anticipates. In trying to touch your toes, for example, the backs of your legs soon call a halt to the stretch that you thought you could do. Tension is felt in the hamstring muscles and the small of the back. A stretch reflex has taken place in which various muscles involved contract in order to prevent overstretching and thus injuring the tissues. The extension of the stretch shows the current limit of flexibility. A consistent but gentle program of exercises can improve flexibility, strengthen the legs and back, and thus prevent the most common injuries of running.

Specific Injuries

According to Dr. David Brody, director of the Runner's Clinic at George Washington University, 30% of running injuries involve the knee. The second most frequent site of injury is the Achilles tendon, with Achilles tendonitis accounting for 20% of injuries. The other frequent injuries are shin splints 15%, stress fractures 15%, and plantar fasciitis 10%. Two other clinical studies of running injuries have reported similar findings. Dr. John Pagliano, a sports podiatrist, and Dr. Douglas Jackson, an orthopedic surgeon, discussed their ten-month study of 1,077 running-related injuries in *Runner's World*. Another study by Dr. D. Cement, Dr. J. Taunton, W. Smart, and K. McNicol, in which 1,650 patients with running injuries were seen over a two-year period, was reported in *The Physician and Sports Medicine*. Both studies showed that the single most common cause of injury was "attempting too much too soon. " That is, runners accelerated from one level of speed or distance to another before the body was able to cope with the progress. Inadequate warm ups, inflexibility of muscles, and improper shoes were also listed as frequent causes of injury. Drs. Pagliano and Jackson found that lightweight runners got injured less often than heavier runners, and that runners who ran on hills developed more injuries than those on level terrain. It is interesting to note that 68% of the subjects in this study were injured doing interval training (short, hard, fast runs interspersed with walking). Twenty-five percent were injured using a combination of these two methods. One of the most surprising statistics showed that the low-mileage runner is the one most frequently injured, while the high-mileage gets hurt infrequently. Perhaps the reason for this infrequency of injury in high-mileage runners lies in the care and planning they usually give their workouts. In contrast, the casual low-mileage runner often tends to be indifferent and inattentive to warm ups, stretches and schedule.

Runner's Knee *(Chondromalacia)*

Runner's knee, or *chondromalacia,* is associated with chronic pain in the region of the kneecap. The pain is felt under and around the patella. There is a tightening or general soreness in the region of the knee joint, usually before or after one runs. Surprisingly, it does not seem to affect one during a run. However, if it is neglected, sooner or later the pain will increase with such sharpness that the runner is unable to work out.

Runner's knee is often the result of ill-fitting shoes or the attempt to increase mileage before the legs are able to withstand additional running. The pain is further aggravated by attempting to run uphill. The complex structure of kneecaps require many different ligaments and muscular attachments for movement. Walking and running involve all these attachments strapped in interdependent ways to four bones. These are the femur (thigh bone), which descends from above; the tibia and fibula (two bones of the lower leg), which ascend from the ankle; and the patella (kneecap), behind which these bones join and forming the area of the knee. The proper running movement of the kneecap and the flexion and extension of the knees require two indispensable factors: first the dynamic balance of muscular strength and flexibility in the legs, and second, correct foot function.

If the four quadriceps, for example, are of unequal strength and flexibility, the kneecap will pull to one side. If the feet are not landing properly due to structural problems, poorly fitting or worn shoes, or poor running posture, the lower leg will rotate abnormally on the femur bone. This pulls the patella to one side and imbalances the strength of the quadriceps. Prolonged imbalance can eventually produce degeneration beneath the patella.

Most runners who have foot dysfunction reveal one of two extremes: high arch or flat feet. Those who have high arch may find relief by landing more on the ball of the foot, where as problems associated with flat feet will need orthopedic aids to accommodate excessive pronation.

The remedies for improving runner's knee have been confirmed from personal experience. I have found three kinds of exercises to strengthen the region and thus prevent irritating soreness. First of all are the stretches and postures listed in the previous chapter, especially the leg lifts. In addition are two exercises that concentrate on the quadriceps muscles supporting the knees; one is isometric and the other isotonic.

1) Sit down in a chair with one leg extended and resting on a pillow about six inches above the floor. Flex the leg muscles as though you were trying to keep the leg rigid. Hold the contraction for 10-15 seconds. Release the contraction, and switch legs. Repeat the isometric contraction with this leg also for 10-15 seconds. Continue to alternate legs this way for 3 minutes. Every 5th day add an additional minute to the total time. This exercise should be done twice daily until the pain is completely gone.

2) The second exercise requires a weight. This may be a sandbag, a plastic pail or a sack filled to weigh approximately 5 to 7 pounds. Sit on the edge of a table or chair, extend one of the legs, place the weight across the top of the ankle and lift the leg until it is parallel to the ground. Lift very slowly and then gradually bring the leg back down to the ground. Start with 5 lifts. Repeat the exercise using the other leg. Do 3 sets of 5 lifts with each leg. Every month add one more set to the exercise.

It is important that these exercises, which were designed to strengthen the muscles and tendons of the leg, be done by both legs so that no imbalance in strength occurs. If you strengthen only one leg, you may cause the same injury to occur in the other leg. It is also important that these exercises be done slowly, so that the mind's attention can be given to that region of the body and thus gain maximum benefit from the contraction/release. During this time the running program should be continued, but no long distance running should be undertaken while there is any pain. The workout should consist of gentle running, 100–400 meters, using these segments combined with long walks to cover the prescribed minutes of the workout. If you attempt to run more than 400 meters, you will irritate the soreness and lengthen recovery time.

Application of ice for 10-15 minutes may reduce inflammation. These should be followed with heat treatments. You may also want to include a series of sit-ups in your workout, to strengthen the abdominal area, since this will lend additional support to the lower part of the body.

Iliotibial Band Friction Syndrome

With some runners a curious pain may emerge along the outer side of the knee during the workout. Continuing to run with it only aggravates the pain, forcing the runner to slow down and finally stop altogether. The pain usually ceases when the running stops. This injury is what is known as iliotibial band friction syndrome. The iliotibial band is an elongated fascia that descends laterally from the hip to its attachment at the tibia. It constantly rubs over the side of the knee as the leg flexes and extends. Since it is unaccustomed to being stretched for long periods, as in running, the area becomes inflamed from overuse. This syndrome may result from hyperpronation (excessive inward rotation of the foot), sudden extra mileage, and ill-fitting shoes. It can be helped by rest and a lighter workout for a day or two, combined with postures that gently stretch the leg, such as the Triangle Pose. I have found the homeopathic remedy, Arnica, to be the most helpful for strained connective tissue, such as the iliotibial band. Ice application may also give relief in more severe cases.

Achilles Tendonitis

Achilles tendonitis is a type of soreness that will not interfere with a normal workout if detected early enough. Achilles tendonitis is characterized by tenderness, often acute, when touching or pressing the tendon near the ankle. One may also notice a tenderness or burning sensation on either side of the tendon. This burning or tenderness is generally felt after a workout or upon rising in the morning and taking your first steps.

The Achilles tendon is really the lower extension of the calf muscle. It is the largest and strongest tendon in the body, connecting the large bulging rear muscles of the lower leg to their anchor in the heel bone. The calf, or gastrosoleus muscle, may suffer cramps, but soreness in that region is mild compared to that of any inflammation of the tendon itself.

The causes that produce this affliction are various: running on hills or uneven terrain, pounding the heels hard when running, suddenly increasing mileage, wearing poorly-fitted shoes, or wearing shoes that have worn down and no longer absorb impact sufficiently. Thus the heel must take a greater strain during the movement of the foot. To counteract this tenderness, stretching exercises must be continued to maintain the flexibility of the calf muscles. Strengthening this muscle comes as a result of the stretching. In our running schedule we indicate the types of exercise that can be used on a daily basis in order to gradually strengthen and maintain the flexibility of the calf muscles.

Through experience, I have discovered another excellent way to relieve the pain and prevent additional injury in the Achilles tendon. This is a simple daily massage of the tendons. Most people might resist this approach, assuming that the tendon is simply too tender to touch. That is partially true; the tendon is indeed very tender with tendonitis. But massage is possible and will relieve pain as well as revitalize the area. Simply place your thumb on one side of the tendon bellow the sore spot. In a gentle, soothing motion, press lightly upon the tendon in an upward motion from the heel bone to the calf muscle. Return again to the other side of the tendon and again press gently upwards. Do this even if there is a feeling of discomfort. Continue this massage for about ten strokes. Then go to the other ankle, for invariably when tendonitis occurs both ankles are involved. Repeat the process and return again to the first foot. Continue the upward stroke with your thumb, but this time you may notice that you can press just a little harder. Continue stroking, but without causing pain. Then, after ten strokes, go over to the other ankle again and do the same. Come back to the first ankle for another ten strokes. Continue to repeat this procedure for 15 minutes, or until the soreness had either been eliminated or is faintly residual. I was very surprised to discover that by increasing the firmness of the massage in proportion to the ability of the tendon to withstand the pressure, I was able to drastically reduce or eliminate all of the pain. Make sure that the pain has vanished before you attempt another run.

In his book, *Running Wild,* Olympic and world record runner Gordon Pirie mentions that he once entered a two-hour contest. Although his longest run in his best condition was 10 miles, he decided to attempt the world record at the longer run. He broke the former record and finished second in the race. But as a result of the strain, his Achilles tendons were so painful that he had to walk stiff legged for weeks. He tried various remedies with negligible success, until some friends recommended a clinic. There his tendons were massaged back to health. The remedy was so painfully administered, however, that he had to grip the table to endure the treatment. Not until four months after the injury occurred could Pirie begin to run again.

Of course treatment by massage should not be so painful. It does not require kneading with great pressure. The pressure should be adjusted to the tolerance of the pain. With further stimulation, the soreness will diminish and the tendon will accept increasing pressure. The tendons, like the knees, have less than abundant blood and nutrients supplied to them. Massage delivers increased circulation into the entire region, thus promoting the diffusion of waste products and accelerating healing.

The tenderness of the Achilles tendons may happen on recurring basis until the legs are sufficiently strengthened from the stretching postures. In that case, the massage should be done daily. What may also help is the use of Arnica, the homeopathic remedy mentioned earlier, which at one time was considered a primary remedy for athletes. Massage with Arnica slave is exceedingly helpful for relief of pain. Another remedy is cold applications to the painful area, followed by gentle stretches. One may also place a heel pad in the shoes to reduce the stress upon the tendon.

Shin Splints

"Shin splints" is the term used variously to describe the inflammation of the lining of the shin bone, of the muscle surrounding it, or the tendons that bind the muscle to the bone. It indicates a repetitive stress on the tibia, or shin bone, the main bone between the knee and the ankle. The shin bone is not "splitting"; rather, there is a feeling of acute tenderness diffused along the edge of the bone and its associated muscles. Shin splints seems to be a protective mechanism of the bone to protect itself from fracture during excessive stress. The muscles in front of the tibia become fatigued, swell, and compress blood vessels, cutting off the needed supply to the leg for running. The tiny muscle fibers which attach the bone lining to the bone begin to pull away from the bone, causing pain.

Shin splints occur due to several causes. Running too hard or too long at the beginning stages of conditioning in a common one. Sometimes pounding on hard surfaces or running on hills causes the injury. Frequently it is a result of tight calf muscles. The injury responds well to a decrease in the intensity and duration of the workout. Running should be done only on level surfaces while treating shin splints, and the running shoes should have proper padding. Application of ice to the area for 10 minutes after running helps the pain, as does an application of Arnica salve with gentle massage.

Here is an exercise specifically designed to strengthen the lower leg and prevent shin splints. Stand erect and place one foot under the edge of a radiator, a bookcase, or heavy bureau so that the foot is raised against the weight. Exert a lifting motion with the foot, as if

trying to lift the object. You will feel a contraction of the lower muscles. Hold the contraction for 5-10 seconds. Release and repeat the
exercise with the other foot. Continue to alternate feet for 1 minute.
Each day add another minute to the cycle until you are performing the
exercise for 5 minutes.

Another way to prevent shin splints is to stretch the calf muscles
daily. The yoga postures most helpful for this are the Ankle Roll, Hand
to Foot Posture, Triangle Posture, Wall Push-Ups, and the Posterior
Stretch.

Stress Fractures

Stress fractures in runners usually occur in the lower leg bones
or the lower spine. As the name implies, the fracture is caused by too
much stress making the bone extremely fatigued. Excessive mileage,
hard surfaces, or training too fast are the major causes. The pain is
similar to that felt in shin splints except that it is usually more local-
ized. If you suspect its presence, visit an orthopedic physician immediately. Further aggravation is dangerous and may prevent running
for months.

Plantar Fasciitis

When the runner feels pain in the heel or the arch, it may be a
case of plantar fasciitis, sometimes called the heel spur syndrome. The
pain may be felt at the beginning of the workout and diminish as the
minutes go by during the run, only to return afterwards. The fascia
comprise a fibrous web or band of tough connective tissue arching
from the heel to the toes. Sudden changes in condition, similar to
those causing the other major injuries, can irritate the fascia sufficiently for it to separate from its connection to the heel bone.
Depending upon severity, treatment involves rest, orthopedic aids,
heel pads, and massage.

The Stitch

Sometimes runners find an unpredictable pain in spite of a sufficient warm up of easy jogging, walking, and stretching. Although it is temporary, it can become intense enough to make you slow down and finally stop the run. It feels like a cramp at the side of the ribs. This is called a "stitch". More often than not the stitch culprit is a faulty breathing pattern: the rhythm of the breath has become erratic or the contraction /expansion movement of the diaphragm during exhalation/inhalation has been reversed. The continued strain upon the diaphragm finally produces the sharp feeling of pain in the ribs.

There are a few things that can be done to relieve the stitch during the workout. First, become more aware of your breath pattern. Make sure that the exhalation/inhalation movements are synchronized correctly with the movement of the diaphragm. The exhalation must be done with the diaphragm moving upward, as the abdomen digresses and moves inward toward the spine. Second, establish even breathing. If you were running at a breath ratio of 2:1, revise the ratio to 1:1. Breathe as evenly as possible and shorten the length of breath for awhile. If you cannot hold the pace, slow down a little until you feel that the revised breathing is now under control and proceeding smoothly. When you adjust the movement of the diaphragm in connection with the revised even breathing, it may take some seconds before you feel a decided relief. Then slowly return to your customary breathing pattern.

Runners have also noticed side pains when they run too soon after a large meal. The remedy is obvious. Allow four hours to elapse after a heavy meal before strenuous running.

Blisters

Blisters seem to sneak up on the runner. In spite of much care, one day s/he is surprised to find a blister on the foot. Blisters are another protective mechanism, resulting from excessive rubbing of the skin. The affected area swells with water under the surface to protect the tissue beneath. If neglected, blisters can become infected.

Blisters will usually heal very quickly with prompt attention. The area should first be cleansed with soap and water. Then the blister should be carefully punctured at the edge and the fluid drained, a clean antiseptic cream should be applied, and the area bandaged. For larger blisters, cut a piece of moleskin to fit around the area, apply salve to the blister, cover with gauze and tape all in place. With this cushioning, running the next day is seldom a problem. To prevent blisters, make sure that socks and shoes fit properly. Keep the shoelaces tight enough for a snug fit. If the feet blister easily, experiment with a full-length foam insole in the shoes.

It is my observation that most leg injuries are the product of a dynamic imbalance. Running will strengthen certain muscle groups at the expense of others. Easy running will stimulate the hamstrings at the backs of the legs, for example, more than the quadriceps at the front. In this situation, the hamstrings become tight and need stretching while the quads become weak and need strengthening. There are two basic ways to restore dynamic balance to the muscles. First, vary the types of running occasionally so that no group of muscles gets developed to the exclusion of others. In a slow easy workout, occasionally introduce high-knee running for short bursts or strides at a moderate speed so that he legs are fully extended. Another approach is to introduce various types of weight exercises to strengthen a specific group of muscles. Homemade weights can often suffice for this task. The extended leg exercise used for knee injuries is an example.

The most essential exercise for balanced muscle groups are the yoga postures. There are no comparable substitutes for the overall benefits of strength and flexibility derived from doing these postures properly and regularly. Even bodies that are structurally impaired can benefit from them with modifications indicated by a competent teacher. It has been my experience that yoga postures never fail to achieve their designed purpose. Runners who fault them generally perform them improperly or fail to do them on both sides of the body as instructed. The basic principle that applies to the execution of every posture is to perform it slowly, with attention, and on both sides, maintaining diaphragmatic breathing. Balanced flexibility that strengthens all the running groups of muscles can be achieved with consistent practice.

If, in spite of these exercises, there is still chronic pain, there may be structural imbalances in the legs, feet, or back. For these problems, it would be best to consult a podiatrist or orthopedic specialist experienced in sports medicine.

Finally, there are some injuries due to overexertion. As your running improves, it is very easy to neglect some steps of the workout. Check yourself occasionally for any of the following symptoms:

1) Inability to maintain the same pace of previous workouts
2) Restless sleep or general irritation and impatience
3) Chronic feeling of tiredness
4) Rapid heart pounding continuing as you slow down or walk
5) Painful labored breathing
6) Drawn appearance or pallor
7) Dizziness
8) Increased stiffness in the legs or constant sore muscles
9) Confusion or uncoordination

Should you find yourself suffering from one of these conditions, stop and reflect on what you are doing to yourself. Sometimes our determination to improve gets ahead of our common sense and our patience. Slow down, refer to the pace of the workout schedule, remember to include the warm up and cooldown, practice some breathing exercises, and the uncomfortable symptoms will soon disappear.

7
Diet and Running

The chief sources of human energy for running are oxygen and
glycogen. Breathing takes care of the former, while the act of
eating supplies the latter. The way we breathe and the food we
eat mainly determine our bodily health and thus provide the continuing resources for running.

The Formation of Energy

Less than half of the energy obtained from eating and the internal processing of food is available to us as usable energy. The rest is
radiated and evaporated as heat, carbon dioxide, and water. When the
bulk of food is processed into glucose (blood sugar) and carried to the
individual cells, some is stored there as ATP (adenosine triphosphate)
molecules, and some remains in the form of stored glycogen (starch).
The liver and the muscles are the primary reservoirs of glycogen.
Although the leg muscles contain glycogen and fats, these are not in
sufficient amounts to last more than a few minutes of running. A normal 30 to 60 minute workout requires that the cells of the leg muscled
be constantly fed, so additional sources of energy are called forth from

the stored glycogen and fats in other regions of the body.

Under normal conditions of running, the body seldom uses proteins in the liberation of energy for movement. Unless the running alone becomes immediately very intensive, research indicates that when the body is undergoing intensive exercise, it prefers almost exclusively the more readily accessible energy of glycogen, which is obtained primarily from carbohydrates. The transference of energy from carbohydrates is more rapid than the burning of fats. In very long distance running, however, (marathons and 50-milers) the processing of fats becomes crucial, since the glycogen stores may be virtually depleted within two hours of running.

Dr. David Costell, in his book *A Scientific Approach to Distance Running,* indicates that in the opening 5 to 10 minutes of long distance running, the body relies upon its glycogen stores in the running muscles and liver. As the runner settles into the run the body begins to depend upon a mixture of carbohydrates and fatty acids in small amounts. But as the run continues, the predominant glycogen reserve becomes depleted, and about 30 minutes later the body prefers to utilize fats through the remaining performance.

It is highly possible that running long distance will train the body to convert fats much easier if the run takes place hours after digestion of the last meal. Nature has composed human bodies so that the reserve of fatty acids far outlasts the carbohydrate reverses. The world-famous physician-coach, Ernst von Aaken, speculates that since women carry more fats in their bodies than men do, they are endowed by nature with the capacity to run better over long distances. A general survey of long-distance races would bear out this observation. In a 100-kilometer race held in Germany in 1976, Christa Vahlensicek finished fourth among 800 men, in 7 hours, 50 minutes, 37 seconds. In a 100-mile race in California in 1971, Natalie Cullimore finished in 16 hours, 11 minutes. None of the male entrants managed to finish the race. In long-distance swimming, women also dominate. Gertrude

Ederle was the first woman to swim across the English Channel. She completed the cross on August 6, 1926 in 14 hours, 35 minutes – 2 hours faster than the cross of the fastest man. In 1977 Cindy Nicholas, a 19-year-old Canadian, swam across the Channel and back in 19 hours, 55 minutes—that's 10 hours, 55 minutes faster than the male record holder!

The metabolism of food for energy requires a continuing supply of oxygen. If you ate the finest diet in the world but ran without the continuing presence of oxygen, the energy output would grind to a halt. If you run too fast, so that the leg muscles outstrip the supply of oxygen, a different, restrictive metabolic cycle occurs: the energy output diminishes. If you attempt to sustain the pace, fatigue and tension accumulate until this new condition forces you to slow down or stop. Anaerobic metabolism emerges. The glycogen turns into lactic acid, drastically reducing the amount of energy available for running. Glycogen stores are no longer converted into sufficient ATP for contraction. Instead, destructive acidity builds up and suffocates the cells and blood. While repetitive running extends the ability to forestall this buildup, as seen in the better conditioning of the body, there is still a short limit of anaerobic running for everyone. Amazingly, the body can later utilize the lactic acid and reconvert it back into glycogen, or even oxidize it completely. The better conditioning you achieve from daily running, the faster this reconversion process takes place. When the glycogen stores are matched with the oxygen supply, as in running in a steady breath state, you have 19 times more energy available than when attempting to run anaerobically.

Dietary Requirements for Runners

A runner does not have to worry about diet in the same way that a ballet dancer might. Yet the eating habits of many runners would cause a scandal in a nutrition classroom. From beer to Cool Whip, runners subscribe to their favorite item, often insisting that it is the secret to their success. Menus of elite runners (Bill Rogers, for example) sometimes include a fourth meal in the middle of the night, when they indulge their fantasy for junk food. Since Mr. Rogers and other marathoners are running twice a day for 15-20 miles, they are probably burning up those pseudo-foods so fast that they hardly stay in the body long enough to do any damage. For the rest of us, however, there are some rules of nutrition that will greatly enhance health and promote running endurance.

Food plays a vital role in our general well-being as well as providing energy for running. The Congressional Committee on Nutrition and Human Needs has stated that the food we eat is directly connected to six of ten leading cause of death in the United States. These are: heart disease, cancer, stroke and hypertension, diabetes, arteriosclerosis, and cirrhosis of the liver. Less disturbing than these fatal illnesses are many of the nagging chronic disorders which we tend to needlessly put up with. These include headaches, insomnia, excessive drowsiness, runny nose, excessive mucus formation, watery eyes, canker sores, sore throat, nausea, flatulence, fatigue, and joint pain. The food we eat and how we eat it is often to blame for these illnesses as well as the more serious ones.

More and more research is showing that while individual needs vary greatly, there are some foods which are bad for everyone and some eating practices which are detrimental to health. All of us at one time or another have experienced the distress caused by eating fried "fast" foods, quickly gulping down food while working, or having a meal of snack food. Afterwards we feel tired or irritable, or develop pain and nausea.

We Americans are infamous for the amount of "junk food" that we consume. Much of our food is heavily processed and filled with chemical preservatives, stabilizers, softeners, and dyes. Researchers are showing that these additives often hinder the natural digestion process, as well as contribute to a number of diseases and behavioral problems. When one embarks upon a program of running, it is not long before one becomes aware of the foods he puts in his body, and begins some healthy questioning. "Is this good for me? Will this interfere with my workout?"

Of special interest to the runner is the use of salt and refined sugar. The average American consumes 15 pounds of salt per year — almost 50 times more than the body needs. The strain on the kidneys due to salt intake contributes to tissue swelling, menstrual pain and high blood pressure, which in turn can contribute to kidney disease, heart attacks and strokes. For the athlete, too much salt in the diet results in a drop in performance. The salt draws water from the muscle cells into the spaces between cells, causing dehydration exactly as salt on sliced cucumbers causes them to become limp an lose their crispness. The athlete and the cucumber both wilt! Runners often use salt tablets when exercising in hot weather. Dr. Robert Arnat, a physician for the United States Olympic Ski team, says that salt tablets dehydrate the body and can cause severe gastrointestinal pain during exercise. He insists that too much salt in hot weather can kill, because salt raises the internal body temperature by interfering with the body's ability to sweat. Since long-distance runners lose large amounts of potassium in hot weather, they would do well to eat a banana before the run. Bananas (and to a lesser degree, oranges and tomatoes) contain relatively large amounts of potassium and can compensate for the loss of potassium in sweating during summer running.

Equally important for preserving health is to stay away from an abundance of that most dangerous of simple carbohydrates, refined sugar. Foods that use sugar (sucrose) as the main ingredient, such as bakery goods, packaged breakfast cereals, soft drinks, candy, ice cream, etc., burden the body even if the food should include some nutrients.

The average American consumes over 120 pounds of sugar per year. Since much of the sugar that we eat is "hidden" in processed foods and drinks, it is important to limit the addition of sugar to the diet. Sugar has no nutritional value of its own snf therefore borrows from the body's reserves those nutrients required for metabolizing it. In this way, eating sugar runs up nutritional "debt" and effects serious imbalances in health. Surprisingly, refined sugar intake is associated with high levels of triglycerides and cholesterol. Like salt, sugar should be treated with reservation.

London's Dr. Ian MacDonald remarks that eating a simple sugar when exercising tends to make the muscles ache by forming lactic acid in the muscles. By eating the complex sugars of carbohydrates in their meals, runners receive energy they need without the handicap of additional soreness.

A Balanced Diet

Running involves the body's use of carbohydrates, fats and proteins, along with vitamins and minerals. A balanced diet that replaces these sources of nutrition is mandatory for the runner. Good nutrition occurs when the above constituents are available in sufficient amounts and proper ratios on a daily basis. No one particular food group should be emphasized to the exclusion of others. Swedish studies on the relationship between glycogen and performance have shown that if you exercise on a predominately protein diet, for example, you may increase the bulk of your exercised muscles, but your endurance will not improve. In fact, it may even decrease to levels lower than before you started the diet. At the same time these studies showed that a fat-rich diet also does not contribute significantly to endurance. Ideally, the mainstay of the runner's diet should be complex carbohydrates. Interestingly, this matches the diet of some of the longest surveying cultures in the world.

Yogi master Swami Rama brings to light some of the dietary practices of the health practitioners of the East in his book, *Holistic Health:*

As described in the ancient manuals, food falls into two different categories: cleansers and nourishers. Fruits have more cleansing value, while vegetables, grains, legumes and dairy products have more nourishing value. On should include both types of food in his diet every day. There should be a balance between solids and liquids. For most this means a diet that consists of about 40% whole grains, 20% beans, 20% vegetables, 15% fruits and raw vegetable salads, and 5% dairy products. During the winter one should eat less fruit because fruit makes one feel cooler. In the summer more fruit and raw vegetables should be taken and the quantity of whole grains should be reduced. In this way one maintains a proper balance.

Carbohydrate Loading

The renewed interest in diet has produced a certain fad among racers: the superglycogen diet. Back in 1967 Swedish physiologists Ostrand and Hultman devised a week-long dietary program whose end result was the abundance of energy available on the 7th day, the day of the race. Since the announcement of this program, modifications have taken place, but the overall scheme is as follows.

About a week before the race, the runner goes through a heavy or fairly exhausting workout. From this stage, instead of eating normal meals, s/he restricts the diet to no-carbohydrate items, or at least as few carbohydrates as possible. Running continues during the week, further depleting the body of carbohydrate reserves. On the 4th day, the abstinence from carbohydrates is reversed. For the next 3 days before the race, the runner increases the carbohydrate intake to the limit of absorption. The theory is that since the body was deprived of carbohydrates to an extreme degree, it can now absorb them in huge amounts, expanding even further its normal capacity. The runner supposedly now has more readily available glycogen for running needs than if s/he had continued the normal diet up to race time.

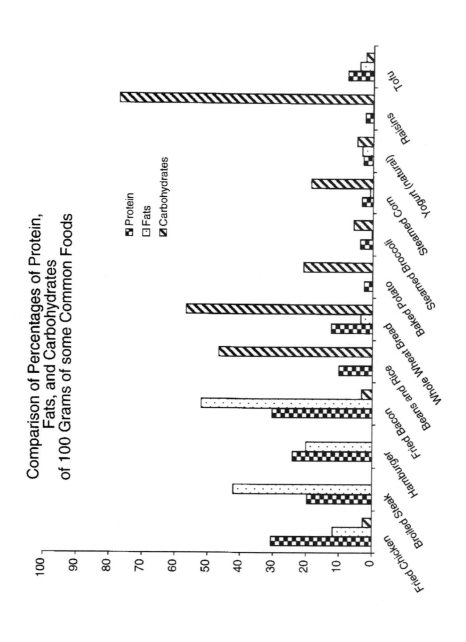

Comparison of Percentages of Protein,
Fats, and Carbohydrates
of 100 Grams of some Common Foods

My own judgment in this matter is that extreme diets are unnecessarily perilous. The superglycogen diet runs the risk of serious injury in many ways. The sudden deprivation of carbohydrates immediately creates an imbalance that is further intensified by running again and again. It is not surprising to learn that runners become very irritable and easily fatigued during this carbohydrate withdrawal. Moreover, the body may be pushed to hard, causing injury to the muscles during the workout. Without the normal glycogen, the runner's overall feeling may affect his or her self-confidence about the upcoming race. It is hard to feel in prime condition if you feel increasingly tired for 3 days in the face of your workouts. You are also vulnerable to illness by acutely lowering your energy reserves. Susceptibility to infection will increase. Among these other imbalances you could be starving the brain, which utilizes carbohydrates primarily for its metabolism. The body is a creature of habit. Rapidly changing one of its main functions, digestion, is an unreasonable gamble to take to win a race.

There is a much safer way to approach the manipulation of glycogen. Two or three days before a race, simply decrease your workout and continue to eat your normal level of carbohydrates. On the race day and even before, you will feel full of energy as a result of the abundance of glycogen.

The enormous, unpredicted interest in running has aroused physiologists to launch research in other areas pertaining to the running body. Both the testimonials of runners and controlled experiments have produced a revision in our understanding of the runner's food requirements. Formerly, many athletes and coaches considered protein as the major source of energy. Athletes would indulge in diets rich of red meat, a steak typically being consumed before the big meet. By mistakenly emphasizing protein rather than carbohydrates, the athletes had less energy readily available and made the metabolic process work harder to get what the runner needed. Carbohydrate is the key nutrient, not protein. Therefore, a runner's diet, like everyone else's, should be predominantly rich in this ingredient.

Vegetarianism

Although runners need not become vegetarians, I would like to offer some encouragement to those runners who have pondered the advantages of altering their menu towards vegetarian principles. Athletes are quite capable of living on a vegetarian diet, as history proves. The famous Finnish runner, Paavo Nurmi, was a vegetarian who set 20 world records and won 12 Olympic medals in the 1920's. The Australian swimmer, Murray Rose, was the youngest Olympic triple gold medal winner up to 1956; he had been a vegetarian since childhood.

Eating wholesome foods should always be the guide, regardless of diet preferences, but there are some definite advantages to increasing plant foods in your diet. First of all, they digest easier than the meat dishes, leaving one feeling lighter. The nutritional values of plants are generally more balanced and higher in carbohydrate energy than meat. A glance at Chart 6 will give an immediate comparison of carbohydrate, fat, and protein content of typical vegetarian and non-vegetarian foods. To get us through the day, the body needs more carbohydrates than proteins or fats. The typical American diet until this century was more balanced along the lines of vegetarianism. In more recent decades, the consumption of meat had become more an international symbol of affluence than a sign of improved nutrition. Studies of people under sudden dietary restrictions, during World War II for example, indicate vastly improved health as a result of virtually meatless, low-protein diets. In most cases, such as those in England and Denmark, whole grains and vegetables replaced meat in the wartime diet.

The runner should be wary of too much red meat. Not only is it more difficult to digest than other forms of plant or grain protein, but much of it surprisingly contains more animal fats than the expected protein. Most people overestimate beef as a source of energy. If you are interested in building endurance, nothing suits the body better than emphasizing an abundance of carbohydrates in preference to huge amounts of meat protein and animal fats.

Fluids

A runner needs more fluids than a sedentary person. The salt and mineral losses from sweating while running are usually replaced by the vegetables of the next meals. The mild dehydration incurred can be replaced by drinking water. Just before running, take a glass of water and immediately after the run, take 1 or 2 more, depending on the warmth of the weather.

Many runners swear by beer. This is, I think, simply a superstition. Alcohol hurts the body by undermining the absorption of B vitamins and traumatizing the nervous system and liver. Since you are trying to replace liquid in the body after running, alcohol has the opposite effect; it produces dehydration. Dr. Jean Ellis remarked to *Runner's World* that "moderate alcohol intake elevates the amount of HDL (high density lipoproteins) in the blood...A high level of HDL reduces the risk of heart attack...In the chronic drinker it (HDL level) is very high. He may have destroyed every organ in his body, but he'll probably never die of a heart attack." I fail to be impressed with the logic of favoring a fluid that is so potentially harmful as to leave only the heart intact. There are much easier ways to elevate HDL levels than choosing alcohol.

Plain water is by far the best fluid replacement, along with freshly squeezed fruit juices. Water immediately helps the body reduce its internal temperature from the heat of running. In hot weather, then, the runner should drink more water than normal.

The drinking of water before running also prevents another problem that has been noted in distance runners. Sometimes the runner will notice dark-colored urine. When one runs with an empty bladder, the continuous motion can produce mild bruising as the bladder bounces. The slight bleeding thus enters into the urine. This solution seems to work every time: drink before you run. The additional liquid apparently cushions the bladder, preventing it from becoming bruised during the workout.

The last recommendation for taking fluids is in regards to meals. If possible, eat your food without imbibing liquids. Liquids dilute the digestive enzymes and cut down on the amount of saliva produced in the mouth. Since saliva aids digestion, your digestion will be faster and more efficient if you refrain from drinking until at least half and hour after a meal.

The question of when to eat in reference to running is often debated. It is better to spread the hours between eating and running as much as possible. One will feel more comfortable, lighter, and ener-getic the longer the time span. If I were concerned about a race, then fasting overnight would be my preference. Generally, the less food being digested the easier it is to run.

Eating late at night is also hard on the body. In the evening the digestive system slows down with the rest of nature. Expecting it to suddenly go to work while the body is sleeping puts a strain on the organs which may show up later in life. Late night eating also makes it very difficult to awake refreshed in the morning, ready for work or a run. The yoga system of health advocates eating the main meal in the early afternoon, while a lighter meal in the early evening and then fasting until morning. Stress to the digestive system due to gulping food, eating while angry or upset should also be avoided. It is simply not worth the trouble. Why put extra strain on the body we are trying to build up?

Although one may not be able to follow this regimen exactly, a good health rule is little or no food after sundown or before sunrise. When we spend so much effort on training and running to enhance our health and prolong life, we would be foolish indeed if we reversed those efforts by consuming poor quality food, eating it improperly, and ignoring the gradual consequences of our faulty diet. We wish to develop a lifelong program of good health with running. Thus we should also pay close attention to the fuel we assimilate from food. We should demand the very best – the freshest, most nutritious foods we can obtain. Our food should be cooked well and combined proportionally to give us optimum benefits. We should really enjoy our food and take time to eat it. Studying our body's interaction with food is one of the principle ways we can add healthy years to our life.

8

Important Considerations

Your future with running will bring discoveries about your body and mind that will surprise you. The ability to enjoy your workout is an experience that should be jealously guarded. It is with that aim in view that these last suggestions and reminders are offered.

Posture

Improved running means relaxed, skillful performance. This implies correct posture. The upper body has two primary functions: breathing and balancing. It is interesting to note that while many people have poor posture while walking casually, the moment their pace becomes brisk, their posture improves. In running the opposite seems to prevail, human bodies differ in their corporeal expression, much like human personalities. Yet there are sufficient similarities in bone and muscular structure to justify some general guidance for efficient movement.

Occasionally one should assess the position of body parts and the way the feet move during the running cycle. Without proper alignment, stress can mount easily, to leave one tired before s/he should be. Distance running is usually more comfortable when the spine is upright, or at a nearly vertical stance from the pelvis to the top of the head. Be careful about the spinal column. Some runners bend their spine backward near the bottom. They make their lower back curve outward, allowing the buttocks to protrude. This puts undue stress upon the lumbar region, producing the pain of swayback, or lordosis. The more relaxed position would have the buttocks tucked under, allowing the pelvis to be forward as though it was being lifted upward. Some runners prefer a slightly forward lean. This is fine as long as the lean does not become acute. If so, there will be pressure on the chest, decreasing the movement for efficient breathing.

The head should be upright, looking forward rather than down. The arms present a problem until one finds an easy, slightly pendulum action. Don't hunch the shoulders; keep them lowered naturally. The chest and shoulders should remain fairly stationary rather than pivot from side to side. The frontal motion of the hands and forearms should slide forward without exaggerated reaching. To prevent the arms from swaying from side to side, and the waste of energy which this causes, don't allow the arms to cross over the center of the chest. In a natural arm swing, the elbows should bend at about a 45-degree angle, and move only a few inches beyond the sides of the body. The hands or wrists may brush slightly against the waistline. Clenched fingers induce stress. A natural, cupping of the fingers slightly streamlines the motion.

Feet should point directly forward in striking the ground. The extension of the legs produces a slightly curved foot which strikes the ground from the outside edge. This implantation happens so quickly that it is difficult to discern. Frontal pictures of runners will reveal this angled stride. Distance runners usually prefer to allow the heel to touch fractionally first before coming down on the rest of the foot. Other runners touch the ground more towards midsole or nearly flat-footed.

Running involves implanting the foot so that the body's weight is distributed from the outside edge inwards and toward the toes. This stabilizing curve from the outside to the inside during foot implantation is called pronation. Weak ankles superpronate, resembling the inward angle seen in beginning ice skaters. If superpronation becomes chronic, then orthotics and a visit to the podiatrist are in order.

The business of moving forward pleasantly and efficiently does not require bouncing on the balls or toes of the feet. The upper body should remain fairly steady and not waste energy by rising and falling. Running from will, no doubt, have individual characteristics that modify the above descriptions, but experimentation should lead eventually to a comfortable and stressless posture. Discovering the feeling of a relaxed posture maximizes the economy of energy, prevents injuries, and produces a motion of fluid beauty.

Winter Running

Winter running can be a lark, as many runners have found. Beginners, however, are sometimes afraid to exercise outdoors during these cold months. Some think that their lungs will freeze. Others are sure they will "catch" a cold or flu. Some fear frostbite. But if you have been running throughout the fall, your body has been gradually acclimatizing itself to cooler weather. The body will make the necessary adjustments to cold weather without much concern provided you take a few precautions.

The nose, for example, is a small heater. Cold air is warmed up by swirling around inside the nasal passages before descending into the lungs. It has been my experience that even in below zero weather the air is sufficiently warmed through nasal breathing. In severe cold winds you may find it helpful to wear a ski mask or a scarf over the nose for the first mile or so of running in order to adjust to the temperature.

Speaking of sharp winds, there is a danger of frostbite if the face or hands are exposed to winds for long periods of time. Before a run in cold, windy weather, cover exposed parts of the face with Vaseline or a protective face cream. This insulation will be adequate for the face, and warm gloves will protect the hands.

Winter air requires a double set of clothing for adequate insulation of the body heat. Of course your winter ensemble is strictly an individual selection, since retention of body heat differs among runners, but many incorporate the following suggestions. Besides the outer garments that you have been wearing thorough the fall, you will probably also need to wear a set of long thermal underwear. As added insulation against the winds and damp air, a windbreaker should suffice. The body loses a great deal of heat – almost 60% - through the top of the head; for this reason, a woolen cap helps.

One can become overheated by being overdressed, however, even in cold weather. For this reason one should experiment with clothing for the area in which you live. You will probably find that multiple thin layers are more efficient than fewer heavy layers. Layers of clothing trap air between them, adding warmth. And of course, with layers, the topmost layer can easily discard if the runner becomes too warm. I find the best material for winter to be wool, because it retains body heat even when wet.

It is easier to adjust to a winter workout if you do some of the warm-up exercises indoors. Running in place, stretching, or use of a stationary bicycle increases the circulation which generates warmth. After about 10 minutes of warm-up, continue the workout outdoors. You will then find the cold to be no problem.

If these few precautions are carefully observed, there is no reason why the runner cannot enjoy his workouts throughout the winter months. Those winters when I have continued to exercise outdoors have been blessed with an absence of colds and flu and an increase of energy for the rest of the day.

Summer Running

Insulation is not a problem as the weather warms. The major burdens for the body in summer running are overheating and dehydration. The body now has to work to stay cool. Running in the heat and humidity taxes the cardiovascular system more than running in the cold. The gradual loss of hydration thickens the blood, making the heart pump harder to cool the body.

Adjusting to warmer weather varies from one runner to the next. Some runners thrive in hot weather; others wilt as the temperature climbs. Running in the early morning or late in the day will enable the latter runners to take advantage of the cooler air at those times. Most runners find that it takes them about two or three weeks to adjust to the heat. Regardless of the time of day, however, summer running requires more ingestion of fluids to replace those lost in perspiration. The best fluid replacement for water loss is water during the day and up to 15 minutes before the workout will not upset the stomach. If your diet is excellent, then your normal meals will replace the other nutrients lost through perspiration.

There are fabrics and styles of running apparel for everyone's taste. Light, comfortable clothing which absorbs perspiration well, such as cotton, will aid the cooling of the body and thus is best suited for use in the heat.

Some Reminders

Enjoyable running is a complex association of many factors including diet, sleep, recreation, and attitude toward exercise. Understanding one's personal requirements is indispensable to overall health. Integrating them properly assures a positive foundation, upon which a physiological and psychological equilibrium may then be sustained for higher performance levels of running that carry over into the rest of one's life. The following ten points are some reminders to help novices develop running and enable them to examine their-progress along the way.

1) Run intelligently.

Understand why you are running. Once you have an overall purpose or goal in mind, then understand how to run in ways that will achieve it. When exposed to strenuous running, the body will adjust over a period of time, provided it's permitted to recover from the exertion. The object of your run is improvement, not a test to see how much can be withstood.

2) Run in a regulated way.

Don't leave your workout to your whim on any particular day, but allow your schedule as befits your conditioning. Warm up properly, that is, take your time even when you want to skip the warm up. There will be days when you do not care to exercise. Cursing yourself or moralizing is not necessary. Wait awhile. Keep walking and jogging for a time. Let the outdoors, the scenery or the atmosphere have its positive effect upon your mood. Ten minutes of continuous and gentle movement can more often than not revive your motivation to run.

3) Run without losing your breath.

You want running to build your endurance, not tear it down. Your pace is an individual thing. Moderate it according to your breath. Don't worry about how fast you are going. It is more important to notice how well you are breathing. The rule of thumb is: can you carry on a conversation easily?

4) Breathe diaphragmatically

Let your abdominal muscles assist the diaphragm to do the work. Synchronize the movement of the diaphragm with your footsteps. Soon the body becomes accustomed to the nasal breathing pattern and its continuance only takes a slight reminder. Breathing diaphragmatically throughout the day reinforces the pattern.

5) Breathe rhythmically

Erratic breathing only upsets the nervous system and makes you tire faster. Set the pace of your running so that your breath cycle falls into rhythm with it. Try to regulate the exhalation/inhalation cycle to a 2:1 ratio. Exhale longer than you inhale. If you cannot breathe in a comfortable, smooth fashion, slow down your pace, breathe evenly, or introduce some walking until you feel like running again.

6) Strive for a relaxed, graceful movement.

The more you strain, the more you impair your improvement. Pushing yourself every day eventually makes the activity repugnant. You will improve more by running easily.

7) Taper off gradually.

If you have run for some minutes and are ready for the shower, bring your breathing and feelings back to a restful state. Don't just go indoors; calm yourself down by walking or slow jogging. Wait until you feel slightly refreshed. Give the body a chance to neutralize any acidic condition before ending the workout. You'll be less sore tomorrow.

8) Listen to pain.

Adjustment to running takes time. The more sedentary the lifestyle, the longer and easier should be the approach to incorporating running into it. Feeling discomfort and running with it is not the same as producing pain. Pain is a sign that an assessment of your running is necessary. When the pain cannot be relieved by additional walking, reducing your workout for a few days, or following the other suggestions mentioned earlier, then professional medical aid is necessary.

9) Stretch before and after.

The more you run, the more you need to stretch. A few minutes of warming up is protection against straining the muscles before they are fully prepared to do their work. Stretching after the workout aids the recovery from the exertion. Circulation improves, the waste products are removed, and the tense muscles relax.

10) Eat well but not often.

Running improves your taste for food but not necessarily your capacity for more. The better quality food that you ingest, the less you will have to eat. Wholesome food and proper cooking allow for a wide spectrum of selections. Obviously, processed products are not as nutritious as natural foods. Drink liberal amounts of water and fresh fruit juices. Remember to run on an empty stomach; keep as long an interval between eating and running as possible.

A final thought for all runners: walking and running is your adventure into promoting wellness. As a runner, you are manifesting an attitude that endorses the possibility of enriched living. As mentioned in *The Wellness Tree*, "For generating abundant vitality you have to orchestrate yur energy with skill, love, and bravery. . . . Life's abundance is ready for your daily enrollment. Your attitude toward yourself is your first tool for wellness. Choose well."

Have a great run!

Bibliography

There are many excellent books on running currently available. Runners tend to read everything in the field that they can get their hands on! My list below is limited to those selected writings that I have returned to again and again for inspiration as well as their practical knowledge.

Books:

Daws, Ron. *The Self-made Olympian*. Mountain View, CA: World Publications, 1977.

Hannus, Matti. *Finnish Running Secrets*. Mountain View, CA: World Publications, 1973.

Lydiard, Arthur with Garth Gilmour. *Running the Lydiard Way*. Mountain View, CA: World Publications, latest edition.

O'Brien, Justin. *The Wellness Tree: The Dynamic Six-Step Program for Promoting Optimal Wellness*. Saint Paul, MN: Yes International Publishers, 2000.

Sheehan, George. *Running and Being*. New York, NY: Simon and Schuster, 1978.

Snell, Peter. *No Bugles, No Drums*. Auckland, New Zealand: Minerva Limited, 1965.

Swami Rama. *A Practical Guide to Holistic Health*. Honesdale, PA: Himalayan Publishers, 1980.

Ullyot, Joan. *Running Free*. NewYork, NY: G.P.Putmanand Sons, 1982.

Periodicals:

Running Times. Wilton, CT: Fitness Publishing Incorporated.

Runner's World. Emmaus, PA: Rodale Press, Inc.

Track and Field News. Mountain View, CA: Track & Field News, Inc.

About Dr. Justin O'Brien

Dr. Justin O'Brien has explored running since he was a little scamp in Chicago. He loved to run! In his paratrooper days, he was Regimental 440 and 880 champion and the last race of his military career found him entering the 2 mile steeplechase "for the fun of it." He claims he saw his past life go before him coming over the last water jump of that race.

Over the years, he has enjoyed conversations with world famous runners and coaches such as Alec Wilson, Emil Zatopek, Gil Dodds, and Arthur Lydiard. He learned much from them. His twenty-four years with the great yoga master, Swami Rama, then turned him into a holistic athlete.

O'Brien is a pioneer in the exploration of wellness. The running/breathing method he created has helped many athletes—from high school cross-country teams and Boston marathoners to international tennis players and Olympic badminton stars.

Former Senior Research Fellow in Holistic Medicine at the University of London Medical School, Director of Education and Stress Management at London's Marylebone Health Clinic, Graduate School Director and faculty of the Himalayan International Institute of Yoga Science and Philosophy, he is now adjunct faculty at the University of Saint Thomas in Saint Paul, the University of Saint Mary in Minneapolis, and Preceptor at the Institute of the Himalayan Tradition.

O'Brien holds a Doctoral degree in the Philosophy of Consciousness and a Doctorandus degree in Theology from Nijmegen University in the Netherlands, Master of Arts degrees in Philosophy and Religious Studies from Marquette University and St. Albert's College in Oakland, California, and undergraduate degrees in the Classics from the University of Notre Dame and Philosophy from St. Albert's. He is also certified in Ericksonian hypnotherapy from the American Hypnosis Training Academy. He is author of several books including *The Wellness Tree* and *Walking with a Himalayan Master*.

Yes International Publishers

Yes International Publishers is the publishing arm
of the Institute of the Himalayan Tradition.
It offers books and tapes in wellness, yoga,
leadership, mysticism, spirituality,
and accessories for practice.

By Justin O'Brien, Ph.D. (Swami Jaidev Bharati)
Walking with a Himalayan Master: An American's Odyssey
The Wellness Tree: The Dynamic Six-Step Program for Creating Wellness
A Meeting of Mystic Paths: Christianity and Yoga
Running and Breathing
Mirrors for Men

By Charles Bates
Pigs Eat Wolves: Going into Partnership with Your Dark Side
Ransoming the Mind: Integration of Yoga and Modern Therapy
Mirrors for Men

By Theresa King
The Spiral Path: Explorations into Women's Spirituality
The Divine Mosaic: Women's Images of the Sacred Other

By Swami Veda Bharati
The Light of Ten Thousand Suns
Subtler than the Subtle: The Upanishad of the White Horse

By Linda Johnsen
The Living Goddess: Reclaiming the Tradition of the Mother of the Universe
Daughters of the Goddess: The Women Saints of India

By Other Authors
Circle of Mysteries: The Women's Rosary Book by Christin Lore Weber
Soulfire: Love Poems in Black & Gold by Alla Renee Bozarth
The Yogi: Portraits of Swami Vishnudevananda by Gopala Krishna
Streams from the Sacred River by Mary Erickson & Betty Kling
Mirrors for Women by Cheryl Wall
Three Paths of Devotion by Prem Prakash

Call our Saint Paul, MN office for a complete catalog:
651-645-6808
For orders only: 1-800-431-1579
www.yespublishers.com

About the Institute
of the Himalayan Tradition

The Institute of the Himalayan Tradition is a non-profit yoga organization for study and sharing, education and community.

It offers residential programs, classes, workshops, conferences, biofeedback, and retreats in holistic transformative training that touch daily lives from the mundane to the sacred, from business to mythology.

These classes are taught and facilitated by experienced teachers who have, in turn, been taught by others, and they by others, in a direct line of spiritual teachers reaching back five thousand years. The rishi who brought these teachings to the United States in 1969 and founded the Institute of the Himalayan Tradition is Sri Swami Rama of the Himalayas.

The Institute offers six teacher training programs in hatha yoga and meditation. Our hatha yoga programs are registered by the Yoga Alliance in both the 200 and 500 hour requirements, ensuring certification for graduates.

An annual yoga conference is held each summer bringing international speakers, teachers, and mystics to share their wisdom and skills.

The Institute of the Himalayan Tradition investigates the essence of spirituality without the necessity for any particular dogma or doctrine. The core of all spiritual teachings of IHT is yoga meditation.

Private consultations in wellness, yoga, leadership, and spirituality are available with IHT main teachers.

Call for information and class schedule:
651-645-1291
www.ihtyoga.org.